Born in the '40s
Raised in the '50s
Died in the '60s

Written by George Brondsema

PublishAmerica
Baltimore

First printing

ISBN: 1-4241-0214-6
PUBLISHED BY PUBLISHAMERICA, LLLP
www.publishamerica.com
Baltimore

Printed in the United States of America

This book is dedicated to my wife, my daughters, my grandchildren, veterans, past, present, and future, and all others whose lives have been touched by war.

Foreword

In this book I have attempted to shed some light on the life of the Vietnam Veteran. I will try to show who they were, where they came from, how they felt at the time, and for those that survived, the impact this war would have on their lives. This is from my own experiences, and observations of others that shared many of the same experiences. I do not want to appear ungrateful in any way for the life that I have been given, beyond my war experience. This is especially true in reference to the families that lost a loved one, and those still coping today with the life altering injury they received in combat. Further, this book was not written as a condemnation of war, but rather to show the affect of war on the human spirit, and to address the casualties that war creates that are never written about. This is by no means meant to be an illustration of the war experience by every individual that participated

For me, this has been a self examination used as a means of therapy. This is a journey through life, from birth to death. It's about families, values, ethics, pride, and patriotism. It is also about pain, suffering, bitterness, coping, and resentment. There is a common thread sewn through us as Veterans, and I hope, and pray that other Veterans will read this, and find a sense of peace in knowing they're not alone.

This book is also for those that were not a part of this era in history, or for those that are interested in learning something about the price of war in human terms. Veterans of this time were often misrepresented, and perhaps in my own way, I am trying to set the record straight. These Veterans were your sons, fathers, uncles, cousins, friends, and neighbors. They were just ordinary young men put in extraordinary conditions. All of them had their own hopes, dreams, and aspirations for a bright future, which was then cut short by a war they didn't create, or lose. For those that survived, life meant going home to fight another war, a war of indifference.

For the families that suffered the greatest loss, know that your loss is shared by others. There are over 58,000 names on a wall in Washington, but just reading these names will tell you nothing about them as individuals. For this kind of insight, you will need to talk to their families, friends, and those that served alongside them. To these people, each and every name represents an unbearable loss.

In the writing of this book, I have deliberately withheld the full names of those I speak about, so as to not intrude into their lives, or the lives of their families.

George Brondsema

Table of Contents

Chapter 1

The '40s

Most of us would have little, if any memory of the '40s. We were born following the end of World War II. Looking back now, it seems ironic that our lives began as a result of war. We would be called the "Baby Boomers."

This was a time in our nation's history where individual possibilities could become realities. It was a celebration of life, and the changing of lifestyles. As a country, we felt a sense of accomplishment, along with a healthy dose of pride, and patriotism. Anything seemed possible, but this is not to say there were no growing pains, and that everyone shared equally in the "American Dream."

In my own case, my parents were the first generation in their families to have been born in this country. Their parents had come to this country to get a piece of they're own American Dream. It's hard to imagine what kind of optimism it must have taken, for so many people to leave the only life they ever knew, and go to a new country. They would have to learn a new language, accept new customs, and do all this with only the clothes on their backs. Then again, they were following a dream. Life may have been difficult, but at least it was their choice to make. For many others already in this country, the choices weren't always within their grasp.

My parents' generation has recently been called "The Greatest Generation." This characterization is not without some justification, although I suspect that if we were able to present this case to all other generations throughout our history, there would be some cause to debate this distinction.

In some ways their choices were more clear-cut. They had been raised in the era of the "Great Depression." I certainly don't mean to imply that this was an easy time for any of them, but basically they had only one direction to go, and that was up. There is something to be said about going through difficult times as a society. The result of sharing this experience together gave them the inner strength, sense of purpose, direction, and courage needed to persevere as a people in difficult times. When World War II came along, these same people had what it takes to get the job done. Individually, and collectively, they would all make many sacrifices before it was over.

When their war was over, a period of adjustment was needed for the various directions their lives would take. I say "Their War," because it seems there has been a war throughout history for every generation that comes along. As for my generation, our war would come later. This is a sobering thought, since I now have children, and grandchildren of my own.

My family's participation in World War II was no different than most other families. My father had served his country in the Navy. He was an Electricians Mate aboard a Destroyer that operated in the Pacific Theater. The term "Theater" seems like a strange term to describe the geographical area of participation in a war. Oh well, leave it to the military to come up with their own language.

My parents were married in 1941, and had two sons born during the war. My mother, like many other women of the time was left to do whatever she could, to hold everything together back at home. Everything at home was built around the war effort. People had to get accustomed to living with rations on such things as food, and gas. Collections were constantly being held for anything that could be used to manufacture war goods, and aid in our ultimate victory. We had to take care of our troops overseas, because winning the war was our only option.

All my uncles also served in various capacities overseas. It would have been difficult to find any family at this time that wasn't doing their part in this massive effort. Whether you were overseas, or at home, this war would touch your life in many ways.

The entertainment industry also did their part to boost the morale of the troops, but also served to rally the efforts being made at home. During this time, many movies were made capturing the heroic efforts of our troops, with the steadfast support of our nation at home. These were images that most young men of my generation grew up with, and embraced as the most noble of causes. This particular view remained prominent in our culture until it was time for "Our War."

Chapter 2

The '50s

I was born in Chicago, but my family moved to the suburbs when I was an infant. This was not unusual for the time, and besides moving to the suburbs, was just another fulfillment of the American Dream. What had once been a rural area, had suddenly now developed into a whole new lifestyle. Suburbs were springing up around all the major cities throughout the country. For the returning World War II Veteran this became a place where he could cut his own piece of the pie, and raise his family. This lifestyle also changed many of the ways families lived up to this point.

We created a whole system of commuters, since most of the jobs were still in the city. Some men drove, while others took trains, or buses to work each day, but the payoff was when they returned home to their "Castle" at the end of the day. The majority of families had one car at this time, and was generally considered the domain of the male.

For the most part, women in this era were stay at home moms. Many of them had never learned to drive a car. Things were changing however, with the move to the suburbs women no longer had the neighborhood to rely upon. There were no corner stores, and public transportation for all practical purposes didn't exist. Extended family members were no longer upstairs, across the hall, or down the street. Just like during the war, they had to be self-sufficient, and independent. Eventually, second cars in the family became more, and more commonplace. This didn't occur in my family until the early '60s. To replace the lack of centralized shopping districts, "Malls" were created, and this became the domain of the female.

Expectations for men, and women were pretty well defined at this time. Men were expected to go to work, bring home a paycheck, fix things that were broken, maintain the cars, and cut the grass. Men were also supposed to be the "Heavy" when it came to discipline. What child didn't tremble at the mere utterance of "Wait till your father gets home." As a result, men at this time were not allowed to display emotions.

Women were assigned the job of everything else. This would include cooking, cleaning, shopping, childcare, taxi driver, routine household maintenance, decorating, budgeting, nurse, and teacher.

When the '50s began, we were barely out of diapers. In a couple short years we started going to school. Everyday at school we began the day with the Pledge of Allegiance. This was our first lesson, outside of home, that taught us something about what was expected from us as American citizens. Patriotism was something you freely showed toward your country, and without any reservations.

At the beginning of this decade, we found ourselves involved in yet another war. This time the whole world wasn't at war, but there was something just as ominous out there, and it was trying to take over the world as we knew it. This time we were in Korea, and the enemy would be something called Communism! We were told that it had to stop it there, or face the risk of it consuming our country, as well as the rest of the world. As small children at this time, we really didn't understand anything about what was going on over there, unless somebody from your immediate family was there, and besides we were told it was way far away. Having learned more about it in later years, I always felt that the men that were sent over there never received the proper recognition they so richly deserved. This was the first time in modern history that men died in a war for their country, without it ever being declared a war. For the twenty years that followed World War II, we as a people have put our military men in harms way against hostile forces from other countries on several occasions, yet we have refused to acknowledge any of these actions as a war. We have instead used other terminology such as "Police Action," or "Conflict." It's as though we couldn't deal with the thought of another war, so by calling it something else, we could make it better somehow. Maybe we simply had a case of feeling so good about ourselves after World War II, that we just didn't want to give that up. After all, those men had fought the good fight in the "Real War." Tell that to the men that fought and died in your name in Korea! To call it anything other than a war, only serves to diminish the heroic actions, and efforts of our Korean Veterans.

After we left Korea, a fear of Communism still persisted. We were also well into the age of nuclear weapons. On the home-front, our schools were routinely conducting drills to protect us in the event of a nuclear attack. They were sort of like fire drills, except that in this case, you didn't go outside. Instead, you went to a basement shelter within the school if you had one, or got under your desk, and tucked your head between your legs while covering your eyes. There were some families that went to the extent of building home bomb shelters. After awhile, I guess we sort of made a truce with this type of thinking. I don't remember exactly when that was, but we just seemed to stop doing it. Actually, sometime later they became the subject of many jokes.

A new thing started appearing in most homes in the mid '50s. It was called "Television," and we couldn't seem to get them fast enough. They had been around for a number of years already, but most people were just getting their first ones during this time. The pictures were bad, and there wasn't very much programming in these early years, but ultimately few things in our society would have a greater impact on our culture.

The atmosphere of growing up in the '50s varied somewhat from place to place. I guess I can only speak about my own personal surroundings. Inner city kids, and those that were brought up in a rural area had a different experience than mine. There were some things that were common among us, despite our differences.

Most families went to church regularly. Respect was more than just the title of a popular song, and was freely given to anyone that would have been considered our elders, or was in a position of authority, such as teachers, policemen, and government officials. You just didn't question their authority. I'm not sure if this was born out of trust, or fear. Perhaps it was a combination of the two. We may have had some rebellious thoughts, but you either kept them to yourself, or only shared them with someone your own age.

Schools were a place where you learned more than just reading, writing, and arithmetic. They were a place of structure, where you learned to live with others within a well-defined set of rules. Any breach of these rules would bring swift retaliation from the teacher, and God forbid this got back to your parents. There were strict dress codes even in the public schools. Girls had to wear dresses, or skirts, and boys had to wear dress slacks, and buttoned shirts with leather shoes. There was no such thing as wearing gym shoes outside of gym class.

We were the first generation brought up with Television,

although at this time you were lucky if you had more than two, to three channels to watch, and you spent a lot of time manipulating an antenna in order to get better reception. The screens were very small, and everything was broadcast in black, and white. Color televisions weren't in most homes until the mid 60s. The shows consisted mostly of variety shows, but as time passed many other types of shows were broadcasted. Later, our generation would be the first to have "Their War" telecast to the whole world.

Time spent outside of school varied with individuals, but as a rule, boys played sports, and built forts, while the girls seemed to be mommies in training, and played with dolls. We, more or less, created our own games to play, and I honestly don't remember ever being bored. Nothing was structured, with the possible exception of Little League.

My friends and I used to ride our bikes out to what would become O'hare Airport. You could park your bike right in front of the terminal, and walk right up to the planes, climb aboard, and even sit in the cockpit. Nobody seemed to mind, as long as we didn't touch anything, and stayed out of the way of the cleaning crew. It was a far different world.

My family had grown to five children during the fifties. This was not very unusual for the time. Larger families seemed to be everywhere, and this became evident when you saw the number of children playing outside on any given block. Many schools had to be built during this time to accommodate the population explosion created by the "Baby Boomers."

I guess we would have been considered "middle class," but I'm not quite sure how that is determined. We had a roof over our head, and food to eat, and my father had a car, but even in a blue collar lifestyle there are some people that seemed to have a little more, or a little less than average.

For most of my fathers working life he had been a truck

driver, or a mechanic. As I said earlier, most of the moms at this time were homemakers. So, there weren't many empty houses during the day. With these larger families, and only one source of income, there wasn't a lot of discretionary money. Some kids that I knew received an allowance from their parents, and usually this was for doing some household chores. I guess the thought behind this was to instill some sort of work ethic. This was money received for work completed. Our family didn't work it this way. Its not that our parents didn't give us some money from time to time, but if you really wanted to earn some money, you went out, and found a way to make some. Girls usually found babysitting as a means to make some money, until they were old enough to get a part-time job in a store, or maybe a restaurant. For boys, there were many other ways to make some money. We cut grass shoveled snow, had paper routes, and did chores for other neighbors. A few guys I knew learned how to caddy on the golf courses. You were only limited by your own creativity. Most of us started doing these various jobs when we were eight, or nine years old.

We weren't sure what occupations we would choose later in life. This was just a way to make some pocket money. I guess we all did some daydreaming about where our life would take us. For some, the thought of being a professional athlete, or a movie star, or a singer, or whatever your dreams were made of, seemed possible through the eyes of a child.

Long as I can remember I always wanted to make a career out of military service. My father had always been my personal hero, and I spent a lot of time asking him what were probably silly questions about his experiences in the service during the war, but he never treated them as being silly. At least he never let on to me. I wanted to travel to far away places, and do interesting things like he had. There was no higher calling as far as I was concerned.

In the mid-fifties we were introduced to a new type of music called "Rock and Roll." Some parents, as well as religious groups were outraged by this new musical style. It had been called the "devils music," and would surely lead young people down the wrong path. This music became a large part of our culture, and was frequently seen in the movies made at that time. The great fear for a parent during this time was that their children would be somehow influenced by this culture of madness, and end up in juvenile hall. Also, about this time we started seeing television shows like American Bandstand, where we got to actually see the performers, along with groups of young people dancing to their music.

Television had come a long way in a very short time. Anyone on television became an instant celebrity, and a household name. Even the adults measured themselves with the people that came into their homes weekly through this medium. For some reason, we as a people placed a great deal of trust in what we were told through this "magic box" in our living rooms. Even the printed word had lost some of its luster to this electronic connection. More people were using TV as a means to keep themselves in touch, and informed as to what was going on in the world around them.

For the younger viewers there was a variety of shows aimed at their interests. All age levels had shows targeted at them. Suddenly, a Mom could just turn on the TV, and there was an instant babysitter. It turned out to be a very convenient diversion. After all, the kids were learning things, plus being entertained at the same time.

There had always been sponsors on radio shows, but television would become a gold mine for somebody wanting to make their products known to the public. No other source could compete with the visual world that TV provided.

As the '50s were coming to an end, our generation was coming of age. We were becoming teenagers. Our interests were changing, as well as our bodies. Things in the world around us were far from peaceful, but at least we weren't involved in a war. We couldn't wait for the '60s to arrive. This would be our decade! We would get a drivers license, and our school career would come to a close. Basically we could do whatever, whenever we wanted. Our futures seemed unlimited.

Chapter 3

The '60s

The sixties began with a great deal of optimism. We had a new young President that made us feel good about ourselves. In his inaugural speech he asked us to examine our role as citizens by saying, "Ask not what your country can do for you, but what you can do for your country."

Having become a teenager at this time was a mixed bag. On one hand, we were going through the typical things that are part of being this age, but we were also being indoctrinated to doing something more with our lives, and this would be for the common good of all mankind. In this sense, we felt an obligation to serve our country in one capacity, or another.

In 1959, my older brother Jim had enlisted in the Navy. I guess his decision was somewhat based on the fact that our father had served in the Navy. In the town where we lived, there were recruiting offices that represented every branch of military service. At the age of thirteen, I started hanging around all of these offices. In retrospect, I was probably seen by these recruiters as some sort of mascot. I decided at this time, that I would choose this path to be my life's calling. As far as I was concerned, there was no higher calling than to serve one's country through military service. The only problem I had to deal with was the fact that I was too young to enlist at this time. Later on, I even went to summer school so that I could graduate a year earlier, and enlist that much sooner. When I got to my third year of high school, and figured that I had enough credits to graduate, the school administration told me this wouldn't be possible, because I didn't have four years of gym class. In a strange twist of fate our new President had implemented what was called a "council on physical fitness," and four years of gym class was now a requirement for graduation. So, I had to wait another full year to fulfill my dream.

In 1962, my brother's ship was off the coast of Cuba. We were told that Russia had been placing missiles in Cuba, which was only ninety miles from our coast. This would be known as the "Cuban Missile Crisis." President Kennedy ordered a blockade of ships around Cuba to prevent any further buildup of missiles. Eventually, the blockade worked, but not without some very difficult negotiations. We were on the brink of perhaps the greatest loss of life the world had ever seen, a Nuclear War.

There was also another area of the world where we just got involved in a new conflict. It was called Vietnam, but it was far away from our coast, and to tell you the truth, most people had never heard of it before. In fact, the majority of people had no idea where it was, and would have difficulty locating it on a world map. At any rate, we really weren't paying much attention to it, and it seemed pretty insignificant.

The world as we knew it changed one afternoon in November. I was in high school in a study hall, when I remember a girl running into the room crying. All that she got out was that the President had been shot in Dallas. A short time later we heard that he died. School was dismissed for the day, and for several days after that. The nation spent much of this time glued to their televisions watching the live coverage of the funeral. In later years, everyone would remember exactly where they were, and what they were doing when they heard the news.

As the story unraveled, we were told that a radical person with some kind of ties to Russia was responsible for the killing. It wasn't long after this that we would witness his assassination live on television. This occurred at the Dallas Police station while he was being moved. Suddenly our world didn't seem quite as simple, as it once was. I think that because of the circumstances surrounding both of these deaths, that we as a nation became more skeptical. For our generation, it was probably the first time that we really looked outside our own lives, and into the world that we were a part of. In the years following this event, we resumed our lives as they were before, but with a little less trust.

This would be a big year for me. I would turn sixteen, and get the much celebrated "Drivers License." This was one of those highly anticipated milestones in life, and I'm sure it is still held in this high regard today. It kind of made you feel that you were transitioning into adulthood, and had finally arrived. The car represented freedom to us, and of course freedom goes hand in hand with responsibility, but we weren't thinking about the latter part. We were consumed with the thought of getting our hands on a car. We would spend countless days dreaming about that ideal, but nevertheless out of touch car that would define who we were. There were fewer choices then, but we eventually aligned ourselves with a particular brand, and model. There were "Chevy People," "Ford People," "Pontiac People," "Dodge People," and there were a few on the edge that wanted something foreign. We looked at these alignments much in the same manner as someone saying they were a Democrat, or a Republican, and we couldn't imagine that this would ever change over the course of our lives. Everyone remembers their first car. They usually weren't the thing made of in dreams, but like learning to walk, the first step is important, and this time you remember it. You also knew what stood between you, and that elusive dream car, and that was a whole lot of money you didn't have. At any rate, a great deal of time was spent cleaning, and polishing this stepping stone in anticipation of the day you're dream would be fulfilled.

In my case, this meant borrowing the "Old Mans Car," because I was a slow walker, and never got any car of my own, until I went into the service, and saved up enough money to buy one on my own. (The preferred method of my Father.)

As people we tend to live our lives in a bubble. We are unaware of the world outside of our own immediate surroundings. This is especially true of younger people. During the sixties many social issues would be coming to the forefront of our lives, and since we were connected to the outside world, by way of instant images on television, we actually started paying attention to them. This is not to say we had a real grasp of how the other half lived, but at least we were able to witness things that previous generations could only try to imagine.

Growing up in an almost all white suburb had insulated me from people of other races, and many other religions. For the most part, my surroundings included only white people whose religion was Protestant, or Catholic, with very few exceptions.

During this time we became exposed to a struggle that others in our own country had been dealing with for hundreds of years. This was one of racial equality. It had always been there, but if you weren't living with it, you didn't have the same understanding that can only come with the experience. This statement also holds true for those sent to fight in a war. Its one thing to be a spectator, but that is quite different from being a participant.

During the fifties, and sixties we saw images of churches

burning, and people being hung because of the color of their skin. There was one incident in particular that stands out in my memory, and that was when a bomb was placed in a church that killed several young girls. Things like this had been going on for many years before, but the difference now was they were witnessed by all of us. Out of these and other incidents, grew a climate that was ready for change.

One thing that always amazed me was the non-violent approach that was taken by the leaders within this movement. We would see people having fire hoses directed at them, having dogs set on them, and being clubbed while peacefully protesting this inequality. Even as these actions were being taken against them, not one attempt was made to raise a hand in anger to those that perpetrated this violence against them. They stood strong, and made the rest of the world stand up, and take notice. I guess the lesson here, is that there is real power in perception.

Although there were many leaders among this movement, one stands out in particular, and this would be Dr. Martin Luther King. He, along with many others showed us how through determination, perseverance, and staying focused on the issues, that change can occur. Later we would lose him to an assassin's bullet. Once again our country would go through a period of skepticism, loss of direction, and hope. We as a people were gradually coming out of our own individual "Bubbles," but we still had a long way to go in learning to live together.

For high school students, this was a time of relative innocence, by comparison to today. It wasn't that we didn't find ways to cause our parents many sleepless nights, but during the first half of the sixties the methods used by teenagers weren't nearly as complicated as they are today. Drugs for recreational purposes did not exist. Alcohol, on the other hand, had been the choice for years. In my surroundings this generally meant attempting to get some beer, although we would take whatever was available. I would venture to say that most of us could come up with an amusing story about how we accomplished this.

I wasn't much of a student, and you could accurately say I got through high school by the skin of my teeth. The teachers said I was too much of a daydreamer that didn't take his studies seriously enough. I don't know if I was bored, or preoccupied with other things, but high school for me, seemed to drag.

It seemed as though that in this part of your life most of your time was spent trying to look older than you were. Looking too young was a curse to be overcome. Boys couldn't wait to shave, and girls couldn't wait to put on makeup. Clothes had to capture an image of maturity. It's funny, but we will ultimately spend the rest of our lives trying to look younger again. Well, we've made a multi-billion dollar business out of it! Maybe 21 is the perfect age for most of us. You're old enough to make your own decisions, but young enough to look good, but then again I don't see many happy 21 year olds either. I guess we all want what we can't have.

For many of us this would be the last time that life would be so simple. This era in innocence was coming to a close. The lives of some of our generation would end in a matter of days, months, or a few short years, and many of us died along with them, at least in spirit.

Chapter 4

A Dream Realized

My time has finally arrived. Vietnam would also make itself known. Prior to this time, our country had been sending advisors there. The first of many combat units would be sent there in 1965. This is not to say we didn't have some casualties during the advisory stage. We had been told that one of our ships had been attacked without provocation, in neutral waters off the coast of Vietnam, and this was the reason given for sending in the combat troops.

At this early stage of our involvement, I was just finishing high school. I decided that I would enlist in the Marine Corps. They had a delayed entry program, where you could enlist up to 120 days before you actually left. You weren't being paid till you actually left, but this time counted for future pay raises. So, this seemed like a perfect way to kick off my military career. Since I was seventeen years old, I had to have parental permission to enlist. My father signed on the dotted line for me, with his only reservation being, that I had broken the family tradition of going into the Navy. I took the oath of enlistment in February, and left exactly 120 days later for boot camp. This gave me three "free" days following graduation from high school.

During the days before I left, I did pretty much the same things that every other high school student was doing at the time. I was only a Marine on paper at this point, and would have to prove myself worthy of the title in boot camp. Still, I already felt a great deal of pride in what I had done, and the thought of not making it all the way through was just something I couldn't comprehend. As kids we had been exposed to only the heroics, and adventure of military life in the movies, and on television. So, for the time being, this was my only point of reference to visualize what was in my future.

As hard as it may seem today, leaving for boot camp in those days wasn't considered much different, than another young person leaving for college. Parents were proud, but tearful, and there were always the jokes directed at you from friends, and family. They usually had something to do with being put on KP, or how you would survive without your mom's home cooking, or who was going to pick up after you now, and sleeping in. Somewhere through this process somebody with a little better idea of what was about to happen, gave you some final advice to shut up, and pay attention! I guess they knew something that we didn't. At any rate, it's probably good advice for many situations you come across in life.

As my 120 days came to a close, my thoughts were on how I would measure up in boot camp. I really wasn't nervous about leaving. Those feelings wouldn't come till I got there. In my case, this was also the first time that I ever flew on a plane anywhere. So, there was a feeling of excitement, and anticipation in making the trip.

When the day arrived, my parents would see me off at the airport. I guess you could say that the atmosphere was fairly typical for most young men in this situation. Coming from Chicago, there was a fairly large group of us flying together. They put one man in charge, and his only function was to carry all our paperwork with him. This was on a regular commercial flight.

As I looked around at the group of people I was traveling with, a thought occurred to me. Even though we were from the same geographical area, we all had come from such different backgrounds. We were White, Black, Hispanic, Oriental, middle class, poor, and were approximately the same ages. I didn't see anybody that appeared rich though. We came in all sizes, and shapes. Some looked as though they could have played football in college, while others looked like they may have a difficult time making it through the physical requirements placed upon them in boot camp.

I wondered if they were here for the same reasons I was. We struck up conversations with each other on the plane, and even though this was an evening flight, and our arrival would be quite late, no one did any sleeping. In the conversations I had, I found that the reasons we were here, were as varied as the differences in our outward appearances. For some, it was a way out of a bad situation at home. For others, it was a stepping stone to getting an education their family couldn't afford. Some had a little trouble with the law, and were given the choice of this, or going to jail. Actually that was a fairly common practice by our judicial system in those days. There were also guys that were drawn here just like me. Whatever reason that brought us together, we would soon have to learn to rely upon each other, and think with a single mind, and purpose. No longer would your individuality matter. Who you were, and where you came from, no longer mattered. This would be where the pot melted.

Chapter 5

Boot Camp

As our plane was making our final approach for landing, the atmosphere among us suddenly became very quiet, and introspective. Thoughts raced through our minds about what has going to happen to us. Was it going to be everything we had imagined? I guess we were just holding on to our last minutes of individuality. Soon our thoughts would not be our own.

When we got off the plane we were met by two very large DI's, (Drill Instructors). Since we were in a commercial airport terminal their demeanor was somewhat cordial. So, we thought that maybe this wasn't going to be too bad after all. Upon leaving the terminal things began to change. Once outside, we were told to line up, and get on the buses for the final leg of our journey. When this was accomplished, the Drill Instructors also boarded the buses. Even though no one was talking, they told us to shut up, and look straight ahead at the back of the persons head in front of you. These, along with all future orders were not negotiable. It was only a short distance to the base, but the whole trip served as an introduction to what was ahead for us. The DI's ran up, and down the aisle of the bus, looking for anyone that dared not to follow their orders. I had always thought my Father could weave swear words together like a poet, but these guys were no amateurs. They got directly in your face, and shouted these words, even if you weren't moving a muscle, and believe me, nobody was.

The bus was now pulling up to the gate of the base where it briefly stopped, and then drove a couple blocks to what appeared to be a large parking lot. Once the bus stopped, another giant of a figure boarded the bus, and immediately told us in no uncertain terms, to get off the bus, and put our feet on the footprints that were painted on the pavement. Apparently we didn't do this fast enough to satisfy him, so he shouted to get back on the bus, and do it again. We did this several more times, and by the last time we had gotten it right, although this meant nearly trampling everyone that stood between you, and those footprints.

It was somewhere around midnight when we arrived, and the next few hours were just a blur. Our heads were shaved, we were given uniforms, we sent the clothes we were wearing from home back, and all this was done in what can best be described as hyper speed. Throughout this indoctrination, there had been both physical and verbal assaults made on all of us. This phase continued till somewhere around three, or four in the morning, at which time we were allowed about one hour of sleep before it all started up again. Hard to imagine, but just a few short days ago I was sitting in high school.

Waking up in the morning began with empty metal garbage cans being hurled into the middle of the room, along with the DI's shouting at the top of their lungs. The rest of the day was pretty much what we had encountered the night before. Everything we did had a purpose, and was on a tight schedule. After all, they only had a couple months to convert us from our past lives into a well-oiled killing machine. Days were spent in, and out of various training exercises, interrupted only very briefly to eat. If there was only one word to describe this experience, it would be discipline. Even in eating, there was discipline, and the same rules applied there. No talking, eat everything they put on your tray, clean it up, and get the hell out! Personal hygiene was also handled in the same fashion. In the mornings there would be a whole group of guys trying to shit, shower, and shave, as they called it, in five minutes. This usually resulted in several men looking like they had their throats slit, because of the cuts they received in attempting to shave under this pressure.

The Marine Corps took rifle qualification very seriously. One entire week was devoted to just this. Some guys in their previous life had spent a lot of time hunting, and thought they knew how to handle a weapon. This previous experience was of no help to them here. In fact, many of the guys that had never fired a weapon before got the best scores. This is usually because the hunters were not taught properly growing up. If you did exactly what they told you, qualification was a breeze, however if you didn't qualify, your remaining time in boot camp was spent as a leper. No doubt, qualification day was a day of intense pressure, and some folded under that pressure. The night before our qualification day, our D.I. kept us up all night. The rationale being, that you would be too tired to be nervous. It must have worked, because only one man in our platoon didn't qualify. Needless to say, his life was hell afterward. They made him walk behind the rest of us, and wear his uniform backwards.

At one time, or another everyone took a beating. Now of course this wasn't officially sanctioned, but was commonplace during this era. Usually you had to personally screw something up to bring this upon yourself, although if they thought your mind wasn't in the right place during some phase of training, a well-placed punch was used to get your attention. In my experience, I made the mistake of talking in a hand to hand combat course. This brought swift punishment

31

from the instructor, and worse yet, I was thrown out of the class, making me highly visible to my D.I. when he came back to pick us up after the class. This resulted in another beating. Did I learn from this? Well, I'm still talking about it forty years after the fact. I do have to say that as our training was winding down, we were growing up in confidence. There was a noticeable change in us as individuals, and as a group.

No longer were we the same group of individuals that arrived here late one night a couple months ago. As we marched from place to place, we saw what appeared to be new arrivals. We wondered if we ever looked that bad. We were also grateful to be looking at it from this point in time, rather than theirs.

On our graduation day we were told exactly what our M.O.S. would be. This stands for (Military Occupation Specialty), or what type of job you would be assigned to, and we were also given our orders for where we would be sent. In these days you weren't given a choice prior to enlistment as to what kind of job you would have, or where you would be sent. Nearly all the training to this point was in preparation to become a basic rifleman in the infantry. Some guys would go on to more specialized schools. Each M.O.S. was given a number. As our senior D.I. read off our numbers we actually laughed at those that were being sent to be anything other than a rifleman. As far as we were concerned that was the only job worth a dam, and it wasn't till much later that we realized the real difference. My number came up as (0311 Basic Rifleman).

Now as to where we were going, that was a pretty simple answer. Most of us were going to (FMF PAC) which stands for Fleet Marine Force Pacific, in other words Vietnam. I was assigned to the 3rd Marine Division. This terminology may be a little confusing for those not familiar with military unit designations, and abbreviations, and as I go along I will try to explain them.

The experience of graduation day gives you the highest sense of pride that you will in all likelihood ever experience throughout the balance of your life. Nothing in life is more intense, and fulfilling at the same time. Just ask anyone that has ever gone through this experience. You are officially considered A United States Marine! Now I don't mean to diminish the experience that others had in other branches of service, but a little well-placed rivalry doesn't hurt.

The day after graduation, we were sent up to another base for advanced infantry training. Just when you thought you were going to get some new found respect, this place turned out to be more of the same. Training was with all sorts of weapons we hadn't used before, so it proved to be interesting. We had grenade training, machine guns, and flame throwers to name a few. Also we were learning tactics on a larger scale. Pretty soon, this too was over.

Soon we would be given a taste of freedom for the first time, since all this began. At this time we were all proud to wear our uniforms away from the base, and couldn't wait to show them off at home. Our only problem is that we legally were considered just kids. In my case I was still seventeen years old, and in the future I would serve two tours of duty in Vietnam, and would still not be able to drink a beer legally. It makes you wonder.

We were now given a twenty day leave to go home. Most of us had never been away from home for this long a period of time. The feeling of going home was almost as great as finishing boot camp. The days at home seemed to fly by, unlike the days spent in boot camp. You felt that you had been gone forever, and had a lot of catching up to do. We wanted to take everything in, because now we were going to be gone for a real long time. For some, this would be the last time their friends, and families would ever see them alive again. Individually, this thought never occurred to us, but may have been in the minds of some of their family members, or friends. After all, we were teenage Marines! What could happen to us? We thought we were invincible.

We left our homes and families with an emotional goodbye. Mine took place at O'hare Airport, but this type of ceremony was being played out all over the country in one form, or another. There were different faces from different places. In a strange way, we were almost embarrassed by all the attention given to us. I think this came from how we perceived ourselves. We were trying very hard to live up to an image.

In later years, I wondered if we had known what was ahead of us, would we have acted differently, and what would we have said to the people that cared so much about us? To the families, and friends, please know how much we really appreciated this outpouring of love, and support. These would be the visions that would sustain us in the days ahead. To the families, and friends that suffered the greatest loss, I can say without reservation, and from experience that your sons talked about this event frequently.

Flying back to the base turned out to be similar to when we left for boot camp. There was a feeling of uncertainty inside, hidden by an exterior of confidence.

Chapter 6

Crossing the Pond

When we arrived back at the base, we were put into a unit called "Staging Battalion." This was kind of like a holding area where they waited until there was a group of Marines large enough to fill out on a plane. Usually you were there a couple of weeks. You also went through some processing for going overseas. This would include getting shots, and filling out some forms. In later years they would also have some additional training in this phase.

Prior to arriving here, we had been with the same people since we entered the service. Here, there were guys from bases all over the country, and they weren't all brand new recruits like us. Some had been in the Marine Corps for many years. We were all going to Vietnam, but would be assigned to various other units once we got there. In previous wars, this process was handled differently. They would send an entire unit that had trained together in the states, and would return home in the same manner. The first groups sent to Vietnam went over in this fashion, but after that everyone was sent as an individual replacement as the units needed them. Each man was to fulfill a specific amount of time over there, and then he would rotate back to the states by himself. In the

Marine Corps, this was a thirteen month tour of duty. The other branches of service chose twelve months. So, even though you were assigned to a specific unit over there, you went there by yourself, and returned by yourself. Your clock started ticking once you left the states.

No other single policy implemented during this time would have such an adverse affect on the future of the Veteran, than this "individual" approach to providing the manpower needed to fight this war. For many, this is where the feeling of isolation began. Here, you weren't even there yet, but you already felt like you were on your own. This was especially true for those of us still in our teens. Going through the trauma that all wars provide is difficult enough, but when there is no one around you to share that experience with, the impact on the individual can be devastating, and last a lifetime.

Everything that we previously had learned about military service showed us there was this band of brothers feeling among military units, but the first thing they did when you finished with your training, was send you off to war, and make you feel you were on your own. It's true that once you got there, you were with the same people, but none of you were going to go home together. This time, more than any other, is when Veterans need the support of their fellow comrades.

When we had the required amount of men to fill the plane, and had completed all the necessary paperwork, and were up to date with all our shots, it was time to go. We left Camp Pendleton, and were driven up to El Toro Marine Air Base on a bus. I just figured we would be flying on some large military aircraft. Much to my surprise, there was a regular commercial airline jet waiting for us, complete with "Stewardesses." They weren't called Flight Attendants at this time. It sure seemed like a strange way to be going off to war, but everything about this war was different than previous wars, with the exception of the war itself. Getting on this plane was more like you were going on a vacation somewhere, rather than a war zone. After boarding the plane, we just sat back for the long flight, and talked to the guys sitting around us. I only knew a few of them from my boot camp days, and we would go in different directions once we got in-country. We made only one stop on the way to Vietnam, and that was for refueling on Wake Island. It was around midnight when we arrived there. They had us get off the plane while it was being refueled, and marched us over to an Air Force mess hall to get something to eat. This was somewhat of a culture shock for me, since most of my experience with eating in the service was in boot camp, where you side-stepped in line, looked straight ahead, didn't talk, and ate everything they threw at you. There was still a line, but this time they asked us how we wanted our steaks, and eggs. Wow, this place even had condiments on the tables, and table cloths! One guy made the comment, "looks like they're trying to fatten us up for the kill." This initially brought a round of laughter, but was followed with a long period of silence.

We got back on the plane for the remainder of our flight. Next stop would be Vietnam. Since none of us had ever been there before, and didn't know what to expect, the mood on the plane varied. I wondered to myself, will it be anything like I imagined, will I measure up, and will I return the same way I left?

The Pilot made an announcement that we were now in Vietnam's airspace, and would be landing shortly. We all strained to look out the window, and get our first glimpse. It actually looked beautiful from the air. When the wheels touched down, and we taxied over to the Danang Airport, another announcement was made "Welcome to Vietnam." Thirteen months would now begin!

Chapter 7

1st Tour 65-66

As we stepped off the plane, we felt a sudden wave of heat, and humidity. The next thing that caught our attention was the pungent odor that filled the air. Somebody said it smelled like death, or rotting flesh. There are some things involved in a war that you just can't comprehend, without actually being there. For people sitting at home watching it unfold on television, you are only experiencing a small part of what war is like. You think by seeing the visual image that you have an understanding of what its like, but in order to truly understand you have to be able to use all your senses. If you talk to Veterans, most of them will tell you that some of their strongest memories aren't the visual ones burned into their memory, but are the smells, the sounds, and the sense of touch that recall a certain place, or experience.

We were brought to a waiting area that was sort of like a tent city. Here we would receive our assignments that would determine who we would serve with, and where we would be going from here. As an infantryman, or "Grunt" as we were called I would be assigned to the 2nd Battalion 3rd Marine Regiment 3rd Marine Division. I was the only one from my group on the plane assigned to this unit. My first night in-country would be spent in this tent city. I was to catch a helicopter the next day, and be taken to where my unit was. Here would be another new experience for me, since I had never flown on a helicopter before. I was really beginning to add up my air miles, and by different means of flight. I didn't sleep much that night, and being next to Danang's Airport didn't help. This facility had more flights going in, and out of it, than any commercial airport back in the states. It was active 24 hours a day. This included everything from a single engine prop plane, to helicopters, to large transport planes, and the most advanced fighter jets of this time.

I kind of gave up on getting any sleep, and just wandered around the compound the rest of the night. All around the compound were sand bag bunkers. I came across a guy that was stationed here, and asked him if they ever saw any action around here. He told me that they occasionally got hit with some mortars, and one time they had been hit with rockets. He seemed pretty nonchalant about it. He asked me who I was being assigned to. So I told him, and all he said as he walked away was "good luck". Off in the distance, I could see some bright flashes in the night sky, and every once in awhile I could hear some rumbling noises. Soon I would be boarding my first helicopter, and wondered what it would be like on the other end of my flight. Training was over, and now this would be the real deal.

The morning sun broke through, and the day began to heat up. It was always hot, and humid, but when the sun rose higher in the sky it became oppressive. As a kid, I had gone to Charleston, South Carolina in July to visit my brother who was stationed there in the Navy, and thought that was hot, but this beat that heat hands down. I wasn't sure if I wanted to leave this place of relative safety, but knew the choice, wasn't mine to make. Somewhere in the early afternoon I got on board the helicopter that was to take me where my unit was.

I was the only person on board, outside of the flight crew. They had also loaded a bunch of mail bags on there with me. When the engine roared, and we slowly started to lift straight up, I thought to myself that riding one of these was sort of like being on a roller coaster. You climbed up, and up, and then you flew forward picking up speed. Once in the air, the view was incredible, plus you had the added dimension of looking straight out into the horizon without any obstructions, since there were no doors where I was sitting.

I don't know how long the flight was, but my heart was pounding heavily in anticipation of what was ahead for me. Would we be under fire when we got there? I thought, Oh God, please don't let me screw anything up out here. This place plays for keeps. I was trying to recall all the smallest of details from my training, but I couldn't concentrate on anything, but where I was, and what I was doing.

Another compound was coming into view, and the crew chief pointed down, and said "welcome to your new home". It turned out that this was only my Battalion's rear Headquarters. It wasn't that much different than the place I just left, except there was no big airfield. Hey, this doesn't look so bad! People were just walking around, and most of them weren't even carrying weapons. Hell, I can deal with this!

I was to become a very short term resident of this compound as well. After all, I was a "Grunt," and this is not where they live. As I got off the helicopter, I was met by a Corporal who told me to follow him to this tent. Inside the tent was an office of sorts. A Lieutenant looked over my orders, and told me I would be assigned to Fox Company, and would be replacing another Marine that was killed. Then he sent me over to another tent to get a rifle, ammunition, and the rest of what I would need. After that I was to go back to the helipad and wait for another helicopter to take me out to where my Company was. They were on an Operation about thirty miles from here. Well, so much for this place. What's next?

The next helicopter arrived, and I threw my gear aboard. They had me, and a few other guys load cases of ammunition, and c-rations to be taken out there with me. Inside the helicopter there was very little room left for me to get on board, but I managed to squeeze in to a small place between the c-rations, and ammunition. Just as with my first helicopter ride, I would be the only person on board that wasn't a part of the crew. Apparently this was a very heavy load, because when the helicopter started to lift off it seemed to be straining under the load. So they sat it back down on the ground, and had to make a decision whether to unload me, or some of the cases. It was decided that I would stay on, and they would make another trip for the cases left behind. There would be many times where they would load up a helicopter with men, and gear, and have to kick some off in order to be able to lift off. It wasn't an exact science, and in some situations it could become deadly. As an example, if you were in the middle of catching some hell in a firefight, and had to evacuate a bunch of wounded, you really had to make some split second decisions as to who went, and who waited for the next helicopter.

The helicopter crews did their absolute best in getting the most out at one time, but they could only do so much. There were other situations where you couldn't get them in at all, due to terrain, weather, or just being under heavy fire. People back home had been told that their boys were only fifteen minutes away from a hospital facility by   helicopter, but in reality this was very rare.

The helicopter finally lifted off, and I was on my way. I had been too busy to think about what was just around the corner, but now those thoughts began to creep up on me. When we got near the area where my Company was set up, we circled around for a few minutes, and then I saw a small cloud of green smoke, which meant that it was safe to land. Well so far so good. Before we even touched the ground, a bunch of guys came running toward us. They dragged me, my gear, and all the cases off in a matter of seconds. Then there were two men running toward us again, but this time they were carrying another man. He had been shot by a sniper, and was still alive, but he didn't look very good to me. They put him on the helicopter, and it took off immediately, but that was the last time we ever saw him.

A Sergeant came over to me, and said "follow me new guy." As we were walking he asked me where I was from "back in the world." I told him Chicago, even though I didn't really live right in Chicago, but in a nearby suburb. As it turned out, this is the way everybody related where they were from. If you didn't live near a big city, then your home state would do. He told me he was from New Orleans, but I guess that could be anywhere near it. Anyway, it seemed odd that we were having this small-talk conversation, about where we were from, after what had just happened. Then again, normal wouldn't be normal over here.

Boys had always been taught to withhold emotions, and it occurs to me that the purpose behind this, originated as a result of their participation in war as men. You cannot function with what war puts in front of you if you get bogged down in emotions. The Sergeant's demeanor was just a way of coping with how he really felt, and for me, this was the first of many situations I would have to learn to deal with. Most people get to go through an entire life without ever seeing someone killed, and the only time they ever see anyone dead is in a funeral home. Normal means something different here.

The Sergeant and I walked over to a few guys sitting on a rice paddy dike. He asked what my name was, and introduced me to these guys. (That one is John, and he is a car nut from Philadelphia, the guy next to him is Jim, he's from New York, and thinks he can sing, and goes by the name of

Nasty Jim, the other guy over there is Patrick, and they call him "the old man," and he is also from New York, and if given the chance, drinks excessively, but there is no one you would rather be in a foxhole with when the shit hits the fan, than Patrick, and by the way you are going to be with Patrick till I tell you different. Pay the fuck attention to him, and do whatever the fuck he tells you, and whatever you do, don't fall asleep on your watch! The rest of us want to get the fuck out of here in one piece! Oh by the way, my name is Ellis, and I already told you where the fuck I was from, and I'm your squad leader. The rest of our Company thinks we're a bunch of shitbirds, but fuck em', who gives a shit anyway?)

I couldn't get over how old these guys looked to me, but found out later they were only three years older than me. They had been in the Marine Corps for a few years already, and were supposed to be discharged soon, but the government extended all their enlistments for six more months so they could complete a full tour in Vietnam. They were part of the original combat landing force that was deployed to Vietnam. In a sense, I felt secure being with these crazy bastards because of their experience. I just wondered if they would be willing to accept a new guy like myself, not that they had a choice, but everyone wants acceptance. This is especially true in a combat zone. Ultimately, they became my family, and at the time we were probably closer than most families.

A lot of Veterans have since told me that they never wanted to get to know anybody over there, because it was easier if you lost someone, but frankly I think this is their way of coping with those losses today, and are not the reality of how they felt back then. You see, those losses are still felt today, and will always be a part of our lives as Veterans.

All that we individually knew about the war was confined to where we were, and who stood alongside us. Most of the time we worked in very small units, or were far enough away from other units so as to not come into contact with them very often. From time to time there had been a few major battles, with large numbers of men in the same area, but most of the time, and most of the war was spent fighting a series of small battles. They were in remote little villages, and on top of nameless hills. The Villages had names, but after awhile they all sounded alike, and they all looked pretty much the same. The hills were only known by the elevation numbers that were printed on our maps.

This was a war of "Grunts" that had little contact with the people who were running the show. Most of our orders were received over a radio, from a voice that we couldn't even match up with a face. It was practically nonexistent for us to ever see anybody above the rank of Captain. We really didn't know anybody outside of our own small circle.

I guess it's about time that I explained something more about the unit sizes, and designations, starting with the smallest, since this is what most Veterans experiences were based upon. First there is a Fire Team=4men, second a Squad=3 fire teams, third is a Platoon=3 squads, fourth is a Company=3 platoons. There were also various other attachments to these groups from Weapons Platoon, such as machine guns, and mortars. We also had a Navy Corpsman or medic attached to each Platoon. Usually we were at about half the strength of what these units called for, and you never got the corresponding rank for the job. There are larger units beginning with the Battalion, then the Regiment, and finally the Division, but understand this is only based upon Marine Corps units. The Army has some different designations.

Now for the rank structure, and starting with the lowest, Private, Private First Class, Lance Corporal, Corporal, Sergeant, Staff Sergeant, Gunnery Sergeant, First Sergeant, Sergeant Major, 2nd Lieutenant, 1st Lieutenant, Captain, Major, Lieutenant Colonel, Colonel. Brigadier General, Major

General, Lieutenant General, General. If you're still confused as to how the unit designations, or rank structures works, then all I can tell you, is see your local Marine Recruiter, and enlist! They will make dam sure you'll never forget the lineup!

It was to become a long war, one that had many participants over the years, but within your own small circle, the faces will always be locked in your memory. We never had the opportunity to see what was called "The Big Picture." We just had a small circle of brothers trying to survive, one minute at a time. I would say day, but too many things can happen in a day.

The Sergeant told us to pack it up, and move toward this tree line off in the distance. This would be where we would set up for the night. As we moved toward our objective, I was apparently hanging too close to Patrick, and he told me to back up, and get off his ass a little bit. He said "what do you want to do, give that sniper out there a group shot at us?" I thought to myself, here I was already screwing up. When we got there, we spread out, and dug in for the night. Then we ate some c-rations. This would be the drill for most every night for the next thirteen months. There were always two men to a hole, and I was with Patrick. While we were eating our chow, I apologized to him for making such a stupid mistake on the way over there. He told me to lighten up kid, you've got a long way to go, and this ain't gonna' be your last fuckup, and besides we all screw up from time to time. I guess it was obvious to him how nervous I was, and his words did help me relax a little bit.

I noticed he wasn't wearing any rank insignia, so I asked him if he was a Corporal. He just grinned, and told me no, he was just a Private. I couldn't believe it, because I already had a stripe ahead of him. He went on to say that he had a few stripes over the years, but always managed to lose them. Over the next few months, I learned all the little things from him that they don't teach you about survival. I also asked him about the guy that they carried to the helicopter when I arrived. He said that he really didn't know him, because he was from one of the other platoons, and he was a new guy.

As a group, we all fell into the belief in superstition, or fate. One common belief was that if you were going to die it either happened when you were a new guy, or as a short-timer getting close to going home. Getting wounded pretty much could happen anytime. Its not that there was no belief in God, because as it has been said before, there are no atheists in a foxhole. Usually the first name called out when somebody is hit, is either God or your Mother.

The days were long, and hot, and it seemed like all they wanted us to do is pack it up everyday, and hike somewhere else. This gets old when you're carrying stuff on your back that is about a third of your own body weight. The nights were spent sitting in a hole, waiting for something to happen, or out on patrol, where you would set up ambushes in an attempt to locate, and kill the enemy. This was our life, and it was punctuated only by someone getting killed or wounded. For some reason we feared mines, and booby traps more than bullets. I think this is because you could be walking along, and get blown into the air, and there was no enemy in sight, and nothing to even shoot back at! With bullets, you had a chance at survival, but with mines or booby traps, if they didn't kill you, than at the very least your body would never be the same again'

Sometimes it felt like we were just walking around with targets on our backs, waiting for the big one to catch up with us. This was a strange war indeed.

A few nights later, I experienced what for me, and many others, would become part of a lifelong nightmare. Our enemy was very adept with the use of mortars. A mortar looks like a piece of pipe or tube, that when you drop a round into it, it shoots up in the air, and then comes down and explodes. They come in various sizes, and can have the impact a grenade or of a small artillery piece. Most of the ones used by the Vietnamese were of the smaller variety, and were very portable. Most of the time, these attacks took place at night. They would see us set up for the night, and just wait for the sun to go down. Any time during the night, when the mood struck them, they would fire off a half dozen rounds at us, or more, and then pick it up, and take off before we could counter with anything. They didn't always hit their mark, but they had a devastating affect on you anyway. They had a very distinctive sound. You would hear each thump as they fired off from the tube, and then it went quiet, till they were angling down toward you. It kind of had a whooshing sound, and no matter where you were, each round sounded like it was going to land directly on your head. Anyone that has ever experienced this will never forget that sound. The use of these weapons remained popular with our enemy throughout the war, and is probably why many Veterans can't stand going to fireworks displays.

In terms of tactics, the Vietnamese were pretty much fighting the war on their own terms. Our problem, at least early on, was that we were using left over tactics from World War II, and Korea. There were no front lines here. There were some areas safer than others, but only because of the fortifications we had built around them. These were our rear areas. We had superior firepower, but were restricted in its use. We also owned the skies with our aircraft, but there again we were restricted in its use. I'm sure our pilots felt the same way we did at times, flying around knowing where they needed to bomb, but were unauthorized to do so, plus they stood the risk of getting shot down. This is fighting with one hand tied behind your back.

It was getting near Christmas, and I asked Patrick if he

thought we would see Bob Hope. He turned to me quickly, and said "Don't even think that!" It seemed like a strange reaction to a simple question. Then he said, "Seeing Bob Hope means you got wounded. Grunts don't get to see USO shows, unless they get shot up, and sent to the rear! Now, do you still want to see him?" Then he laughed and said "How bout a front row seat, then you'll know your ass got shot up real good, and you can show the folks at home your better side!"

Holidays for us, weren't much different than any other day we spent there, except that on a few of them, like Christmas, and Thanksgiving they would bring real food out to us, and it was even hot. Every other day, we had a steady diet of c-rations, and a lot of times these would be eaten cold. The problem was, that after your stomach was used to eating c-rations for months at a time, if you ate anything different it went right through you, but it was good going down. For those unaware of what c-rations were, basically they were just canned food items with such appetizing names as Ham and Lima Beans, Beans, and Franks, Ham and Eggs Chopped, and Beefsteak. These individual meals came in a small box that had a few other things included with them, such as canned fruit, canned crackers with peanut butter, and disc like piece of candy that resembled a hockey puck. Also included were salt, pepper, a very small roll of toilet paper which would be a hot commodity, and a small pack of cigarettes (4) that were like the ones they used to give away on commercial airlines in those days.

Speaking of cigarettes, I had never been a smoker prior to going to Vietnam. The circumstances of how I became one, was kind of unique. Most of the terrain we spent time in was very wet. It included very broad expanses of rice fields, or very thick jungle-like vegetation. In these kinds of areas leeches are everywhere, and no matter what you did to prevent it, they found a way to attach themselves to you. I remember seeing one guy that fell asleep with his mouth open, and awoke to find a leech attached to his tongue. There was no end to where you would find them on your body, or one of your body cavities. It wasn't that they hurt you, but it left an open wound that could get infected later. There was a small bottle of inspect repellent they gave us, and that would get them off, but we rarely ever had enough of it. The most common way, was to hold a cigarette next to them. So, when I had some leeches on me, I would go around borrowing cigarettes from the smokers to burn them off. Eventually they got tired of this, and told me to get my own cigarette. So I did, and that's when I became a smoker. Hopefully I'll be able to quit one of these days, but until them I'm ready for any leeches that come my way.

The government must have had a lot of these c-rations stockpiled somewhere, because the ones we were eating in the sixties were made in the forties. We laughed when we read the label, because a lot of this stuff was older than we were. It wasn't till around 1967 that we used up the old supply, and started eating ones that were made in the sixties. Some guys got fairly creative about adding various spices and other items to make them more appealing. Most of these items they had received from home, while others were acquired in any number of ways.

Water was all around us, but it wasn't exactly pure, or cool. They gave us some tablets that supposedly purified the water, but left it with an iodine-like taste, and we didn't always have these. So we took water from any source we could find. When you are that thirsty you will drink most anything. As a result, dysentery, and diarrhea became a close companion to many of us. The shortage of toilet paper added another dimension to this. Simple things like this you take for granted everyday of your life, but here they took on a whole new meaning.

The word "hygiene" would have been a foreign concept

here. Brushing your teeth for example, was practically nonexistent. Even if you had a tooth brush, you couldn't keep it clean, and probably didn't have toothpaste anyway. In later years many of us had to have extensive dental work completed. Shaving was risky, because of the chance of an open cut, and you didn't want to waste the water anyway. Bathing was done on rare occasions, and usually in a river, or stream if you had soap, and of course this water wasn't exactly pure either.

The clothes we had were never properly cleaned, if at all. Every so often we would get supplied with new ones, and throw the old ones away. Socks and boots were a high priority, but sometimes your feet would stay wet for weeks at a time, and you developed jungle rot. Usually it started on your feet or legs, but was not limited to these areas alone. Later, on my second tour, I got such a bad case of this that they seriously talked about amputating one of my feet. Its one thing to lose a limb to combat, but to lose it to infection seemed ridiculous in this modern era, and by the way, they don't give you a Purple Heart for it either.

On the days we got our mail, and somebody was lucky enough to get a package from home, this would be cause for celebration. Some guys had written home, and asked that certain things be sent, and they may have seemed like odd requests to the people at home. Some things didn't hold up very well, because of the time it took to get there, or the climate once it arrived. The packages were shared by all. All mail was important to us, but these packages were valuable. Of course, everyone didn't always receive some good news from home, and since this was a possibility for any of us, we were willing

I had been in Vietnam a few months now, and was no longer the new guy. There had been a number of guys that had come over since I got here. People were always coming, and going here as a result of getting killed, or wounded, and the ones that survived would rotate back home again. In those first few months, I had witnessed a number of deaths, and injuries. In one instance, while on patrol, a man stepped on a mine, and lost both of his legs. This same mine also wounded six or seven other guys. I don't know what causes people to react the way they do, but there was a Platoon Sergeant in our Company that pulled a pin on a grenade, and found that it had malfunctioned, and in a split second threw himself on it to protect the men around him. He died as a result, and was awarded the Medal of Honor Posthumously. No one sets out to be a hero, and no one can predict what they will do in every circumstance. It is just a reaction to a situation.

For me, this was a difficult time, because now all the guys that were there when I got there were either gone already, or would be going home soon. Fortunately, Patrick, Nasty Jim, John, and Ellis all went home together. These guys had a lot of attitude, and despite their crusty exterior, all of them had a heart of pure gold. I was grateful to have known them, and never forgot what they had taught me. One funny thing happened on the day before they left. They promoted Patrick to Private First Class, and nobody laughed harder than him. He said, "You know what PFC really stands for don't you?" "Private Fuckin' Civilian!"

Shortly after these guys left, the Lieutenant told me that I was going to a different unit. I asked him why me? He said they were forming these small specialized units, and he couldn't send a new guy, and that I would fit in this slot. Then he told me that since my "shitbird" buddies had left, and since their attitude rubbed off on me, I would be the perfect candidate, and off I went. Before I left, they promoted me to Lance Corporal. It's a good thing Patrick wasn't here to see this, because I would have caught hell from him. In his mind, stripes were for assholes.

The unit that I was sent to was called "Combined Action

Company", or CAC. Later they changed the name to "Combined Action Platoon", or CAP. The reason for the name change was that in the Vietnamese language, CAC referred to a part of the male anatomy, and was somehow overlooked, or got lost in the translation. At least that's what I've been told.

What they did here was place a Squad of Marines, and a Corpsman in an outpost to act as security, and advisors to the locals. We would be supplemented by two squads of Vietnamese Popular Forces, which were like their local militia. In some ways it would be easy duty, but if the shit hit the fan, it might be a long time before you got any help, since there wasn't anybody near us for miles. So, this small group was pretty much on their own.

Our little corner of the world was by an old church, alongside what I would laughingly call a highway. There wasn't much left of the old church, just two walls, and part of a roof. There was a small stream about a hundred yards away. We spent the next few days trying to make it home, although the first order of business was to make it more secure. This meant filling a lot of sandbags, and putting up barbed wire around the perimeter

The Popular Forces that were assigned to us kind of moved around at their own pace, and we were never quite sure what they were thinking. Some of them could speak a little bit of English, but not too much. French had always been their second language, because they had been occupied by France for many years. Somehow we would have to learn to communicate with them, because our lives may depend on it sometime in the future. One of them came up to me, and tried to start up a conversion, and he probably could speak the most English, but it was still difficult, and I couldn't get over how he looked, he had freckles all over his face, which was unusual for the Vietnamese. Maybe he had a little French in him. At any rate, we called him "Freckles." He seemed friendly enough, and certainly took the first step in introductions. I guess our greatest fear was whether, or not we could trust them. Up to this point we never had much to do with the locals, and felt with some justification, that underneath they were the enemy.

As time went by we got to know each other better. Our days were spent patrolling our little region, which consisted of a few rice fields, and a few small villages between them. I think we gained the trust of some of the Villagers, but it was hard to say. When we stopped in the villages often times we gave them food, and some minor medical treatment. Sometimes they would invite us to share their food with us, but I really couldn't handle much of it, and only ate a small amount of rice to be polite.

During this time I had become best of friends with a guy from North Carolina named John. He was a soft spoken, small framed man, and was much shorter than me. So, as was the custom, he was known as "Little John." He was a Corporal, and had been in the Marine Corps for over three years. He was married, and had an infant son at home. We spent many hours talking about things like family, cars, food, and what we would do once we got home. We both decided we wanted to buy a sports car when we got home, even if they weren't practical, and he always talked about his Mama's home cooking. This was probably one of the more typical conversations that you would hear no matter where you were in Vietnam. It was about home, and what you were going to do once you got back there.

It seems like you always want what you can't have, and no where else in life, does this ring truer, than in a combat zone. We would spend endless hours talking about food for example. Since we came from all over the country, and covered every race, and ethnic background, the focus on what we wanted wasn't always the same. For some, it was as simple as a fast food cheeseburger, and you would have given a months pay to get one. Others dreamed of spaghetti, and meat balls, or pizza, for others it was sweet potato pie, banana pudding, and macaroni, and cheese. Another favorite was a nice big steak, and some just wanted pancakes. Of course which was best would be open for debate. I would have to say that no matter which was your favorite, Mama's home cooking would usually win out. To tell you the truth, after awhile they all sounded good to me, even if it was something I never had before. These guys made a strong case for their favorite food.

Another subject of conversation was music. Most people use music as a means to remember things. An example of this would be, that was the big song that they played at my prom, or I was doing this or that when I first heard that song played. Just as with the food, the tastes were endless. Being where we were, kind of limited what we heard. Even with a radio, all we could usually get was Armed Forces Radio. They started coming out with battery operated tape recorders, and record players during this period of time, and as new guys arrived, they would be a good source of finding out what was happening in the music world.

I have always held the belief that all types of music can be good to listen to, if they're done well. Now this is where music and food are completely different. Some people aren't willing to try anything different. So, I guess you could say that music was even more of a personal choice than food was. If I had to vote at that time, my personal favorite would have been R&B. I was a huge fan of anything that came out of Motown, and had been since high school. There were many other great labels as well recording this style of music. To name a few, Atlantic, Reprise, Stax, Chess, and I apologize for any others that I may have overlooked. Our musical choices were varied, but on many occasions it was the glue that held us together during the most difficult of times. I really don't think these

Musical Artists ever realized what a major contribution they made for us, and how it lifted us up, so we could hang on, and handle what we had to face on an everyday basis. It may be a little late, but I would like to Thank Each And Every One of Them! A little music will carry you a long way. God Bless!

It was getting well into the monsoon season now, and it seemed as though the rain would never stop. Our little stream had turned into a raging torrent, and our whole compound was surrounded by water. Living on an island was real isolation, but some of the locals, had brought a few home made canoes over so that we could get around. One afternoon, I watched as three of our Vietnamese troops got into one of these canoes, and pushed off. They barely got a hundred yards away, and the boat capsized. One of them made it back to shore, one went under, and I couldn't see him, the third one was struggling in the water, and apparently he couldn't swim, so I jumped in the water, and swam to where he was, and pulled him back to shore. This guy we called "Droopy," because he always looked tired. His eyes were wide open, but he looked relieved that he had survived. We didn't find the other guy that went down till much later.

Sometime later, after the water went down, and everything went back to normal, we were attacked one night. A small group of Viet Cong had come through an opening in our barbed wire. We were able to repel the attack, and killed everyone that broke through our perimeter, except one, and that one was Droopy! Apparently, when he wasn't with us, he was working against us as a Viet Cong. Freckles, along with some others, were holding him, screaming at him, and slapping him around. We weren't sure what was going on initially, but then Freckles told us he was a VC, and that he had cut the wire, and directed the others inside our perimeter. He told us they would handle their own, and we weren't quite sure what that meant. Freckles went back over to him, grabbed him by the arm, and threw him to the ground, and shot him in the head. Then he spit on him, and kicked him. Whether this was right, or wrong, it made us trust some of them at least.

Little John, and I were due to rotate back to the states together, and we were getting to be a couple short-timers now. We talked a great deal about how we would get together back in the states, and buy those sports cars, and at the very least, we would stay in touch with each other, and visit from time to time.

Every so often we had to go get some supplies from the rear, and we took turns doing this. You sort of made a day out of it, and saw how the other half lived. It was his turn, but he told me to go instead, because he just wanted to hang around that day. So I left, and did my usual thing in the rear. When I returned, Freckles was the first person I saw, and something seemed wrong. He was crying, and trying to tell me something at the same time, and I couldn't understand him at first. Then he pulled himself together enough to say "John Dead". By this time the other guys came running over to tell me what had happened. He was out on patrol, and started to walk into a hooch (house) in one of our little villages, and a booby trap, or mine exploded. Little John was killed instantly, and a large part of me died along with him. He was a man small in size, but huge in heart, and I will always miss him.

It wasn't long after we lost Little John that the brass decided to abandon this position. Those of us remaining went back to our original units. I went back to my old unit, but this time they assigned me to Golf Company. They were still constantly on the move doing the same things they were doing when I left. They had a name for us, and they used to call us "Rent a Battalion", because we were what they called a floating battalion, which meant wherever the action heated up, and another unit needed reinforcements, that is where we were sent. We were part of the 3rd Marine Division, but at times we were attached to units of the 1st and 5th Marine Divisions. Over time, we had been in all the areas of Vietnam covered by the Marine Corps. We had been to Hue city, Khe Sanh, Dong Ha, ConThien, Danang, Chu Lai, Phu Bai, Camp Carroll, AnHoa, and everything in between.

I didn't know anybody in Golf Company when I got there, and I didn't particularly like being moved again, but it wasn't up to me, and hell I'm a short-timer anyway. Some of the guys thought I was a new guy in country, and one even tried to feed me a line of shit about being in-country. He was here two months, and I had been here nearly thirteen. He shut up real quick after I told him that.

I was assigned to 2nd Platoon, and made a team leader. Just about the same time that I got back here, another guy had arrived from the states. He was a huge black kid from Tennessee. He must have been about six foot five, and weighed about 240 pounds. He was assigned to my fire team, and since his size was obvious, he became known as "Big Charles." He was really a gentle giant, but I don't think you would ever want to piss him off. I think he just turned eighteen years old, and I was nineteen at this point. Like all new guys, he just wanted to fit in, not screw up, and survive. He did absolutely without question, everything I told him to do. He kind of reminded me of me when I arrived, and hung onto Patrick in the same way.

Earlier in the book I referred to the saying that there were no atheists in a foxhole. Well, there are no racists either. If one good thing came out of Vietnam this was it. We were given the rarest of opportunities, something we would never have experienced back in the states, and that was looking at each other as equals. It's a shame it takes something like this to make you see the value in other people.

Well, I was really getting to be a short-timer now, but these were the times you worried most. We were out on an operation as usual, and my thirteen month calendar clicked, but nothing happened They must have forgot about me, because I was there nearly fourteen months before they sent me home, and my first leg of that journey was riding shotgun on a truck convoy from Dong Ha back to Danang where I would board the Freedom Bird.

On the way back to Danang, I rode on the lead truck manning a machine gun. We followed the winding dirt road through the countryside, and only one thought entered my mind, and that was we were going to get ambushed, or at the very least drive over a mine. I was about short as a short-timer can be. In fact, I was overdue! Guys were always coming up with descriptions as to how short a time they had left. Some examples of this were, I would talk to you, but I'm so short I wouldn't have time to complete a sentence, or I'm so short I can tie my boots standing up. The descriptions were endless, and if you had two short-timers together, it could become quite competitive. One thing we all worried about was getting killed on your last day in country. To this point, I was still alive, and hadn't even been wounded, but I wasn't sure my good fortune would last.

The convoy seemed to go on forever, but when Danang came into view, I breathed a little easier, but I wasn't out of the woods yet. Before the trucks got to where they were going, they dropped me off at the processing place where I spent my first night in-country. This time the place looked like a palace to me. I ended staying here for a couple more days, but that wasn't too bad. At least I was done eating c-rations, and trying to find water to drink, and I never thought the sight of an outhouse would look so good, but when you've doing your business in the bush for so long this place looked like a five star hotel. Imagine, some guys got to spend their entire tour of duty here.

Then the thought of what I had seen since I had been here

started to sink in. I wanted to think about home, but all I could think about was here, and the guys I had served with. So many died, or were wounded. I thought, why them, and not me? I should be happy, but I'm not, instead I'm feeling guilty for leaving. Would Big Charles be ok now, and will he make the trip home like this, or will he be one of the many others whose life was lost? No answers for these questions now.

When my day finally arrived, I was looking over my orders to see where I would be stationed. So there it was, a Naval Air Station near San Francisco. Oh well, put that on hold for awhile, I'm going home first. Now I know there wasn't going to be any brass band waiting for me, but I at least thought people would treat me with some well-deserved respect. I had fought for my country, and would now be able to stand alongside others from previous generations that had done the same.

I was all packed, and walked out to the airfield, where I saw the most beautiful sight I had seen in nearly fourteen months. It was a large commercial airline jet. As I was standing in line to board it, I saw someone in front of me that looked vaguely familiar. I spoke to him, and he turned around, and we both couldn't believe our eyes. It was a guy named Larry that I had gone to high school with. Here we were a million miles from home, and we met up at this time, and in this place. Larry had only been in Vietnam for a couple months, but was being sent home because of a hardship in his family. He had enlisted about six months after I came here.

When we boarded the plane we would sit together for the flight home. Boarding the plane was bizarre. Here a few days ago I was in the middle of it all, and now I was boarding this. It took on a carnival-like atmosphere. The Pilot was at the top of the stairs, and welcomed each of us as we passed him. Once inside we were greeted by a couple Stewardesses. None of us had seen an American girl since we arrived in Vietnam, at least not one without a military uniform. We just stared at them initially. I guess we just didn't know what to say to them, or were intimidated. After taking our seats, they closed the door, and everything was pretty quiet. The engines roared, and we began to move toward the runway. All of us were looking nervously out the window. We were cleared for take off, and taxied down the runway. As soon as the wheels lifted off one of the Stewardesses made an announcement that our next stop would be Alaska. The noise we made was deafening. Everybody on the plane was cheering, and yelling.

It's a very long flight, and most of us were exhausted, but there wouldn't be any sleeping on this flight. Larry and I talked all through the trip. He told me about all the guys that we had hung around with in high school that had also enlisted. We talked about going out some night once we got home, but we never did.

When we landed in Alaska for refueling, we got off the plane for a short time, and just stretched our legs a bit. Here it was mid-December, and we were in Alaska, and we were all wearing jungle fatigues. Dam it felt cold, but nobody was complaining, and we got back on the plane, and took off again. Next stop would be El Toro Marine Air Base in California.

Chapter 8

Welcome Home to the "Divided" States of America

Although this was a long flight, and the second leg of the journey was shorter than the first, it seemed like it would never end. No doubt, it had something to do with all the anticipation that had been building up. As we made our final approach to El Toro our hearts were pounding faster, and faster, yet there was a numbness that we felt, and didn't understand. When we touched down another group yell took over the plane. We wondered if there was going to be a welcoming formation for us, since this was a military facility. The plane taxied over toward a large hanger, and then stopped. The engines shut down, and before they opened the door, we were all standing in the aisles. As we came off the plane there was one man standing at the bottom of the stairs. There was no one else in sight. This man told us to go over to the hanger, where we would have to get checked through customs. After this we were assigned to a temporary barracks. The next day we once again had to have all our paperwork checked out. When this was completed we were allowed to leave for home. We were given a thirty day leave.

Since everybody lived in different places all over the country, we left in small groups, and found the appropriate means of transportation to our destination. In my case, this meant taking a bus to the airport in L.A., where I would book a flight to Chicago. There were a few others going in the same general direction as Larry, and I, and we all stuck together. Outside of the flight back home, this would be the first time in a long time that I wasn't on a base, or out in the bush.

When we got to the airport in L.A. we went inside, bought our tickets, and basically people watched. I had flown into this Airport three times before, but something seemed different to me this time. Maybe it was us, because we really had been gone a long time. We saw people of our own ages, but they looked a lot different to us. The British Invasion of music, and culture had made its mark on current fashions. Boys started growing their hair a little longer before we left, but it was conservative compared to what we were seeing now. The clothes they were wearing looked sloppy to us, but then again we were used to seeing everybody in a uniform. Then again, we probably looked foreign to them with our high and tight haircuts, and neatly pressed uniforms.

We thought somebody would come up to us, and maybe strike up a conversation, but that never happened. Oh well, maybe we were expecting too much. We figured things would be different once we got on our own home turf. After all, California was always a little different from the rest of the country. Maybe it was the Hollywood thing, or the beach culture. No matter, we were heading home, and that can't be bad

When we boarded the plane for Chicago, I noticed that it had a small lounge in the back of the plane with two rows of seats together. I told the guys we should go grab that, so we could all sit together. So we just kept to ourselves on the flight home. One of the guys was 21 years old, and bought a bottle of whiskey at the airport. So we cracked it open, and drank a few toasts to ourselves and to the ones that would never make the trip the way we were, and to the ones that were still there. I guess we got a little rowdy on the plane, and a Stewardess asked us to hold it down. We complied with the request. Hell, we were used to following orders, and the rest of the flight we talked about what we were going to do when we got home.

I thought it would be a good idea to not tell anyone what day I was coming home, so I never notified anyone. I just wanted to surprise them. When we landed in Chicago, Larry, and I were the only ones that lived nearby, and the others had to make connecting flights elsewhere, so we said goodbye, and good luck to them. Larry called somebody to pick him up at the airport, and asked if I wanted a ride, and I said no I can make it from here. Actually I wanted to be alone when I first walked up to my house, so I took a cab.

I jumped in a cab at the airport, and the cabdriver asked me where I wanted to go. All I told him was home, and he laughed for a minute, and then he said "I figured that much, but where is your home?" Once we pulled out of the airport, things started looking familiar to me. I only lived a couple miles from here, so it wouldn't take too long. It was a sunny day even though there were several inches of snow on the ground. Everywhere you looked, you could see Christmas Decorations.

The cab turned the corner on to our street, and then I saw what I was looking for. He pulled into the driveway, and I dug in my pockets for money to pay the man. As I stepped out of the cab, I saw my mother look out the window. She ran barefoot all the way through the snow to where I was standing. As we were walking into the house, she asked me why didn't you call us, and I teased her by saying I would go back out, and call her. She said "don't you dare." My father wasn't home from work yet, but would be home soon. My younger brother, and sister were at school, and they would also be home soon. So, as each one of them came home I got to pull off another surprise. My mother asked me what I wanted for dinner, and I said it really didn't matter. The rest of the night we just stayed home. My mother was on the phone nonstop with all the relatives telling them about today. One of my older brothers came over to the house with his wife, and joined us. I wished that my other brother could have been there, but he lived in Charleston, South Carolina, and that wasn't just down the street.

We stayed up late talking, and when I could no longer keep my eyes open, I went to bed. The next day I awoke lying in a bed in my parent's house! This was a strange feeling, since a few days ago I was sleeping in a hole in the ground half way around the world. I looked around the room, and it was like I had never left. I had slept in this very room for many years, and it had never felt better than this. Not only was I here, but I was also in one piece, and didn't even have a scar on me, at least not one that you could see.

I went downstairs, and everybody else was already awake. Apparently I had attempted to make up for all the lost sleep in one night. My mother made me a big breakfast, and we just talked some more. I told her that I wanted to go out later, and see if I could catch up with some of my old friends, but this seemed to upset her. She just didn't want me out of her sight for the time being, plus she had already invited some of my relatives to come over, and see me that night. I went back upstairs, and took a long hot shower, since this was one of those things I used to dream about. I got dressed, and came back downstairs, and the first thing my mother asked me was "where is your uniform?" I told her that I had been in uniform in one form or another long enough, and wanted to feel how the other half lived for a change. She understood this, but made me promise to put it back on later when all the relatives came over. That night I was going to be on display, but went along with it for my mother's sake.

64

The next day the pressure was off, and I went out for awhile to see if I could find any of my old friends. I had looked forward to doing this for a long time, but once we got together, everything seemed unfamiliar to me. I was like a total stranger in a room full of close friends. The conversation was strained, and we didn't have much in common anymore. We were all 19 years old, but I felt a lot older. I left, and wandered around for a little while trying to figure where else I could go. Then I remembered a friend of mine from high school was due home from Marine Corp boot camp. I went over to his house to see if he got home yet. Hell, we would at least have something to talk about!

I pulled up to his parent's house, and rang the doorbell. There standing in front of me, was the most beautiful young girl that I had ever seen. She seemed a little bit nervous, but was also very shy. Apparently my friends little sister grew up while I was overseas. She told me her brother hadn't gotten home yet, but was due any day now. Her parents weren't home, but she asked me to come in, and wait, because her parents would also want to see me. We sat there, and talked till her parents got home. Maybe because she was my friend's sister, and he was also in the service, and her father was a disabled Veteran from World War II, but she actually seemed interested in what I had to say. Her name was Patty, and she was only fifteen years old at the time, and here I was 19, which is a big difference at those ages, plus I had a lot of miles behind me already. No, I didn't rob the cradle, but later she would become my wife.

My thirty day leave flew by, as you would expect. So, now I flew to San Francisco. It was January of 1967, and at this time San Francisco was not the place to be, if you were in the service. It's a beautiful city, but this was really the center of the anti-war movement in the country. The country had changed since I was gone, and as returning Veterans, we just didn't fit into the scheme of things.

I reported in to my new duty station, and found that I was going to be part of the base security. It was a Naval Air Station, but they had a small detachment of Marines that guarded the base. It was sort of like being a live-in Police Officer. You would be assigned to one of three eight hour shifts, and these would rotate periodically. We stood guard at the gates to the base, as well as other areas within the base. We also had a small jail or "brig" as they were called. Most of the time the brig held prisoners that were servicemen that managed to get themselves in a little trouble. If they had gotten arrested for something more serious, they would be transferred to a long term facility. We usually didn't keep anybody there for more than a couple days. We would also get called off the base, if a serviceman got into trouble in town. Another part of our job included going on funeral details for men that had gotten killed in Vietnam, and were from this area. This part of the job was one of the hardest things I would ever have to do.

One of the first things I was told after I arrived was that it probably wasn't a good idea to wear your uniform anywhere off the base, unless you had to for official business. This was a foreign concept to me, having been raised in an era that valued its servicemen. They said you probably weren't in any danger, but you didn't want to call attention to yourself either. We were told to try to avoid confrontation with the civilians. Going into town wasn't too bad, if you stayed relatively close to the base. If however, you wandered off into some of the areas of the city, or near the colleges, you might be walking into trouble. I got more warnings about how I should act here, than what I had received the whole time I was in Vietnam. Just what the hell country am I in?

There was no way for us to blend into the woodwork either. This was impossible, if for no other reason our haircuts would be a dead giveaway. We stood out like a sore thumb in an era of long flowing hair. Some of our guys actually went to the extent of buying wigs in order to fit in off the base. We also couldn't wear the same type of civilian clothing off, or on the base. We were the guards, but somehow we felt like the inmates! Here we had fought for our country, and we weren't even welcomed to be a part of it.

Up to this point, my only experience in the Marine Corps was boot camp, and Vietnam. This place was like standing around as a little tin soldier with all the spit, and polish, and I understood that doing this was a necessary evil, and I followed my orders, but I hated this place, and on more than one level.

Soon I began drinking heavily to numb myself to the world that existed around me. The funny part of this is that I had to get other guys that were over 21 to buy me the booze, since I was legally under the age to do it myself. I went out, and bought myself a brand new car with the money I had saved up while I was in Vietnam. I don't know if "Little John" would have approved, but I bought myself a Volkswagen Bug. It was green, with a tan interior. I had looked at some sports cars, but they were out of my reach financially. Any way, it was new, it was mine, and it got great gas mileage. At this time I was making $134 a month, so I didn't need any added financial pressure. When I originally enlisted, pay was $78 a month. For the rest of the time I spent here, my free time consisted of sitting in my car, drinking, and listening to the radio. By the way, I did upgrade the radio, and had five speakers installed, along with what they called a "reverb" unit. Once again, the music carried me to a different place, but even the music being that was being played was different than it once was.

There was a song that had as part of its lyrics, "Be the first one on your block to have your boy come home in a box." Of course this was considered a satirical look at the war in Vietnam, but I often wondered if the author of this song ever knew, or cared how this might sound to the Mother of a serviceman killed in Vietnam. Some thing that was also widely used in the lyrics of songs, were references to the use of drugs. The country and particularly the younger people didn't give a dam about anybody, or anything unless it fit into their own agenda. Everything was open for ridicule. Maybe this is why I stuck with my old R&B, because they didn't put out this crap.

Change, for the sake of change isn't necessarily a good thing. There are a lot of people in this world with good intentions, but good intentions don't always produce good results. To our peers, and a large segment of society, our involvement in Vietnam was morally wrong, and the leaders of our country were corrupt. So, there were many well organized protests held throughout the country to protest our involvement in the war. Maybe it was the intent of these people to bring an end to the war, but I believe it only prolonged it, by making our leaders choose to fight it in a way that would ultimately extend it.

Now, the only people left to deal with its consequences are the Veterans, and their families, and they alone have had to live with this legacy every day of their life since then. The Politicians, and Protesters have gone on with their lives, and a few of them have even written books about what we did in Vietnam, but neither of them ever had a clue as to what we went through, or seemed to care about it either. It seems strange that in a country where we have many rights, and the freedom to pursue them, that the Veterans alone are responsible for giving them to us. The freedom of speech and the right to assemble are two in particular that they loved to use, yet they took out their misguided anger at the very people that gave them the right to do so in the first place.

I tried to get a transfer from here to another base, but was unsuccessful. I had two, and a half years left on my enlistment, and I couldn't imagine being here for the rest of that time. Normally, if you re-enlist for more years they will give you a choice of duty, and where you would like to be stationed, but I was not in the service long enough at this point to consider this option.

My life seemed to be in a downward spiral, and I had to do something about it. I went to see our Sergeant Major. This is the highest rank that you can attain as an enlisted man, and one of his jobs was that of a counselor to his enlisted subordinates. This particular man had been in the Marine Corps for 34 years at this time. He was a colorful character, and easy to talk to. He was here just finishing out his career and looking forward to some well-deserved time with his hobby of fishing. We talked for quite awhile about a lot of different things. He had been Corporal of the Guard at Pearl Harbor when it was bombed. So, he had a lot of experience, and history behind him. I told him that I didn't want to stay with this kind of duty, and that I felt I was headed for trouble if I didn't change. He told me it's hard for a young Marine to come to a place like this, if their only previous experience had been in a combat zone. He went on to say that they should only bring guys right out of boot camp to duty like this, but that was impossible, and impractical. Then he told me I was a "Field Marine," and probably wouldn't be happy anywhere else either. I told him I would be better off back in Vietnam. He told me, "Well, we can arrange that with no problem." They were sending three guys a month from here to Vietnam, and oddly enough I may have to go anyway sometime in the future. Whether, or not this would ever happen, I just told him to put me down on the next group of three that were leaving, and he asked me if I was sure this is what I wanted to do. I told him I didn't think I had any better chance of living here, than I did over there. I had only been back in the states for six months, and I was heading back to Vietnam. I was in the next group of three.

The hardest thing I had to do was tell everyone at home that I was going back to Vietnam. You see, I never told them much about what was going on in my life. How in the world would anybody else understand this? Was I crazy, or did I have a death wish? During this time I developed in to quite an actor, and have remained one most of my life since. I have since told my wife that I should have gotten an Academy Award for acting like everything was ok, when in reality I was on the brink of collapse. It just wasn't in the makeup for Veterans to share their feelings with anyone, and it would be many more years before this would change, and then it would only be done in the company of other Veterans.

It took me a couple days aided by liquid courage to get up enough guts to call home, and tell them where I was going. When I got on the phone I only told them half of the truth. First I told them I would be coming home on leave again, and this was met with a jubilant cheer. Then I told them I was going back to Vietnam, and this brought disbelief, and outrage. I couldn't bring myself to tell them that I had volunteered for this over the phone, and figured I would deal with that part of it when I got home on leave.

I packed up the few belongings I had into my Volkswagen, checked out of the base with my new set of orders, and started heading east on Interstate 80. By now I was in a real hurry to get home for two reasons. One was that I felt guilty about not telling them the whole truth, and the other was because I just wanted to get in as much time at home as I could before I had to leave again. Also my family was flying down to South Carolina to visit my brother, and I was going to go with them. The only thing that stood in front of me, were a lot of miles to cover before I got there. I drove straight through, without sleep from San Francisco to Chicago in 38 hours. When I finally arrived I felt exhausted, but couldn't fall asleep right away, but when I did, I was unconscious for about fifteen hours.

Apparently nobody wanted to upset me when I first got

there, so we really didn't discuss it till after I slept. When I finally woke up it was time to face the music, and I wasn't looking forward to it. Now I had to tell the Woman that ran through the snow barefoot to hug me six month ago that I had signed on the dotted line for this. Patty had come over to the house, and was present for this, along with the rest of the family. They had thought the government had done this to me, and that it was unfair to send me back, especially this soon. I told them what I had done, but really never gave them an honest answer as to what made me do this. I'm not sure any explanation that I made would have justified what I had done anyway. I guess it was a good thing that I at least told them this much, because my mother was seriously thinking about calling a Congressman to complain about it. Can you imagine how that would have come out? Once the shock of this settled down, we just tried to make the best of the time we had together, but I would always feel guilty to everyone for putting them through this once again.

We did fly to South Carolina, and Patty went along with us. In hindsight, the fact that her parents let her go with was a huge vote of confidence in me, although we would be under the scrutiny of my parents throughout the trip. I was still 19, but she had just turned 16 a few months ago. We had a great time going to the beach, and taking in the sights, and this was Patty's first time flying. My father had pulled off a funny deal. We had a little difficulty getting all the airline tickets we needed, and when he complained to the ticket agent about it, the agent saw a small gold cross on his lapel, and said "I'll put you all in first class Reverend." "Reverend?" He said nothing.

Since the "Reverend" managed to get us all first class tickets for the price of coach, we made the trip in high style. The airlines gave you a meal in flight anyway, but in first class we had steak and champaign. This is still talked about on occasion today. He just smiled, and said nothing.

Time was running out, and I would soon have to leave again. This time I had a better idea of what awaited me on the other end. I thought briefly, maybe I'll luck out, and get a job in the rear. Hell, it happened for some people, maybe this would be my turn. Who am I kidding, I was a Grunt before, and would probably be a Grunt again. I did wonder what unit I would be assigned to though, but that I wouldn't find out till I got back in-country.

When the day came to leave again, I felt sorry for everybody, but myself. The situation that I had put them in put a strained look on all of their faces. I was responsible for doing this again to the people that cared about me most. You never knew if you would ever see them again, and this could be their last memory of you.

Once again I was packed up, and ready to go to the airport. My father drove Patty, and I, along with the rest of the family to the airport. Being the age I am now, I can't imagine how they must have felt, but they couldn't imagine what was going through my mind either. We parked the car, and everybody followed me as I checked my bag in, then we went to the gate, and waited till it was time to board the plane. When that time came, the only people that weren't crying were my Father, and I. Its not that we didn't feel like it, but men didn't do those things. After being hugged, and kissed by everyone else, I walked onto the plane. Once aboard, I got a seat that faced the terminal, and could see them all holding each other up.

This type of scene was played out thousands of times all over the country, and if you never had to deal with this experience, consider yourself very fortunate. This is one of many situations that every Veteran and his family would have to endure. The next twelve, or thirteen months would be spent praying that they didn't receive a knock on the door with the accompanying telegram.

Chapter 9

2nd Tour 67-68

As I looked around the plane, I noticed that everyone was wearing brightly colored shirts, and dresses. The Stewardesses were passing out flowered necklaces to everyone. This was a special Hawaiian Luau flight from Chicago. It was scheduled to fly to Los Angeles, and then on to Hawaii, but there were a few of us getting off in LA. It was like a big party throughout the trip. All these people were looking forward to spending some time in "Paradise," and were celebrating. A person next to me asked if I was going to Hawaii to be stationed there. I said no, I'm going back to Vietnam. That was the end of the conversation that I had for the remainder of the flight. By this time nobody wanted to hear about Vietnam, and I kind of felt like a leper in a room full of beautiful people.

We landed in LA, and I got off the plane wondering what it would have been like to be one of those that went on to Hawaii. I got on a bus, and went back to the base. Here I was, back in Staging Battalion again. Well, at least I wouldn't be by myself, and would have something in common with the people around me.

There was only one thing that made me different here, and that was I was the only one that had already done this before.

For everyone else, this was their first trip. Processing was a little different this time. Rather than just getting your shots, and paperwork completed they were putting the men through a little additional training. They had this one small area that was supposed to resemble a Vietnamese village, complete with booby traps. Since I had been there before, they put me in charge of this facility. I was given practically no instructions as to what I was supposed to do, other than to run groups of guys through it. I guess this was a brand new thing, and maybe they weren't too sure themselves. On one side there was a set of bleachers, where they would sit while I explained what we were going to do here. Then I was supposed to walk them through it, and show them how everything worked.

They sent a guy with a jeep to pick me up early in the morning, and take me out to this area where I would wait for the groups to arrive. It was still dark, and there was nobody out there, but me. When the sun was coming up, I could see a bunch of buses headed toward me. I really didn't know what they expected of me, and just figured I would make it up as I went along. This village really didn't look anything like what I had seen overseas, and the various booby traps didn't either, but maybe I would be able to convey something to these people about Vietnam.

I never had any experience in public speaking, other than getting up in front of the class in high school. So, when the first group arrived for my class I was pretty nervous. Two buses pulled up, and much to my horror they were filled with nothing but Officers. Here I was just a Lance Corporal at the time, and everyone getting off these buses, were Lieutenants, Captains, Majors, and even a few Colonels. They all filed into the bleachers, and waited for me to begin. I only remember two things I told them that day. The first being "Welcome," and "I never realized the Marine Corps thought I needed so much supervision." They apparently got a big kick out of that, because I got a roar of laughter, and a standing ovation. Well, at least it broke the ice for me. The second thing I tried to convey to them was to listen to the people that were already there regardless of rank, because no amount of training is a substitute for experience. This also brought a positive response in the form of applause. Everything else that day, and in the short time I spent doing this before I went overseas, is just a blur.

I have to say that starting out with that first audience made the rest of them seem easier. For the remainder of time I was in staging battalion, this would be my job. I must have done something right, because I was promoted here from Lance Corporal to Corporal. It was even suggested that I remain here, instead of going back overseas, but when the time came, I was replaced by a career Staff Sergeant, and sent on my way.

Once everybody had completed the process in Staging Battalion, and we had a large enough group, we went to El Toro Marine Air Base and boarded a plane for Vietnam. From here on out everything was pretty much the same as the first time I did this. There was one distinction however, I had an idea of what was coming, and everyone else aboard the plane was like I was the first time. It was strange, but I was treated with somewhat of a celebrity status while we were heading there. Word had gotten around the plane that I had been there before, and suddenly all these guys were coming up to me to ask questions. I probably would have done the same thing on my first trip, but there was nobody on that flight that had ever been there before. Some of the guys asked if it were possible that they would be shooting at us as we got off the plane, and if that were the case, what should they do. A couple of them told me that they hoped we would be assigned to the same unit when we got there. I guess they figured if I had gone through a whole tour as a Grunt before, and came home without a scratch, that I must be lucky, and maybe that would rub off on them too. I was nineteen years old at this time, and so were a lot of the other guys on this plane, but I felt like I was much older, and maybe I was. There were even some career men that had been in for many years already, but this was their first experience with this, and I don't think they were much better off than the young ones that just got out of boot camp.

I'm not sure if I was better, or worse off than the people that accompanied me on this plane. Sometimes not knowing is an easier way to go, because you don't really have a mental picture to draw upon. For me, I think I probably felt more apprehension this time, because I was still filled with fresh memories. As odd as it may seem, the idea of not surviving this tour ever entered my mind, until I had all these conversations on the plane. I almost wished I had kept to myself, because now I couldn't think of anything else.

The flight was pretty much the same otherwise, and as we were coming in for a landing I looked around, and wondered who of these people won't make it through their tour. They were all looking out the window just as I had done the first time. This would be their first view of Vietnam.

Another thought that crept into my mind, was that this trip shouldn't have been necessary in the first place. I really felt then, as I do now, that this war could have been won during my first tour. It was as though we were being sent to fight in a war with one hand tied behind our backs. The North Vietnamese had been fighting this war completely on their own terms, without regard to rules, boundaries, or borders, while we were following some kind of unrealistic rules, or guidelines. The war was being played as if it were a board game, and only our side had to follow the rules. I am in no way trying to justify this war, or any other war. Those decisions have to be made before you send in the first man. Once that decision is made, it is incumbent upon this Nation's leaders to have a plan in place to end the war as quickly, and efficiently as possible, and with the minimum loss of life. Quoting, and observing the Geneva Convention isn't of much consolation to the troops or their families, when only one side adheres to it. War, unlike most things in life, is pretty much a black and white issue. Really, the only gray area exists in determining whether, or not to participate in one in the first place. The leaders of this nation need to understand this, before they make such a commitment.

When the plane touched down, I swallowed hard, and waited for the door to open. When this happened, I smelled Vietnam again, and felt the rush of hot humid air, and felt like I had never left. Just as I said earlier in this book, you use all your senses when it comes to war, and there is a sixth sense, and that one is fear. When I think of Vietnam today, I can still call upon all of these senses.

Just like last time, we filed off the plane, and were brought over to the processing area. I still didn't know what unit I would be assigned to, and was kind of curious to find out. As was the case on the first trip, everyone on the plane was sent to a different unit, and would be going in different directions. When it was my turn to go over my paperwork, I saw some familiar numbers listed after my name. Out of all the units that I could have been assigned to, I was going back to the same Battalion that I had just left only months ago. Once again I would be boarding a helicopter for transportation out to where my unit was. This time the rear area for my Battalion was aboard an Aircraft Carrier. We were still a floating Battalion, and I already knew exactly what that meant. Send them in, wherever, and whenever somebody needs them. Actually we should have been called the "Orphan" Battalion, instead of Rent a Battalion, because we never had a permanent home.

So, I was flown out to the ship, and joined up with my unit.

As was usually the case, everybody was out in the field, and only the rear support troops were here. Basically, these were the people that took care of the administrative part of our unit. So I knew I wouldn't be here long. Now I was assigned to Golf Company, the very same company that I was with when I left the last time. I left my bags, and was issued a rifle, and all the other necessary gear, and got on board another helicopter to take me out to where the troops were.

I was flown out to another small nameless hill where they were set up for the night, along with some supplies, and ammunition. When I got off the helicopter, there standing right in front of me was "Big Charles." He had made it this far, and I was happy to see him. He looked at me with his eyes wide open, and just started shouting "Hell No, Hell No, Hell No, I can't believe what I'm seeing, this can't be happenin', you ain't really here again"! All the time he was saying that, he was walking away from me. I guess I scared him. He was getting to be a short-timer now, and seeing me there, in his mind, meant they could send him back again too. I tried to calm his fears by telling him that I volunteered for this, and although it was possible to be sent back again, it was very unlikely. He told me I was one crazy son of a bitch for coming back, because it had gotten a whole lot worse over here. He said they had just about gotten wiped out on some hill fights back in April. It was good to see him again, but it was even better to see him go home a month later. When he left, he told me he loved me like a brother, but that he hoped he never saw me again. I have thought about him many times over the years since, and prayed that his life has been good. Maybe one day, I'll be able to find him again, and hopefully this time he'll be glad to see me.

I reported in to the Company Commander, and was assigned to the 2nd Platoon.

This was unbelievable, since that was who I was with

when I left. Then I went to check in with our Lieutenant who was the Platoon Commander. He assigned me to be a Squad Leader, and we went over to where my guys were dug in along the perimeter. Big Charles was in my Squad, and he kind of let the other guys know who I was. I think they took some comfort in knowing this wasn't my first trip around the block. Very often, they would send a guy over fresh from the states with no experience over here, and by virtue of the rank he held, he was given the corresponding job. This could create some problems for both the man, and his subordinates. As I told the Officers back in Staging Battalion, the best advice I can give you is to listen, and learn. Most guys did this naturally, but there were always a few that figured they knew everything before they got there.

Probably the most difficult position for a person to transition into would be that of a Lieutenant. Since most of the time in Vietnam was spent working in small units, they would very often be the only Officer present, and were ultimately in charge of everybody that they worked with. Most of these Lieutenants came here right out of Officers Candidate School (the equivalent of boot camp for officers). So in terms of time in the service, most of them wouldn't have much more than that of a Private. In most cases they would turn to their Corporals and Sergeants for advice, till they got their feet wet.

As was the case on my first tour, we would spend countless days going on patrols, setting up ambushes, participating in search, and destroy missions, and then moving to another area to do it all over again. In some cases we fought for the same piece of real estate more than once. We would lose people fighting for it the first time, and lose more when we had to do it again. We were always on an Operation somewhere, and they gave names like "Starlight," or "Fortress Sentry," or "Pegasus." Half the time we didn't know when one ended, and another one began. We never knew exactly what time it was, or day of the week. The only thing important here was your thirteen month clock. Even though we were all working as a group, we were still here on an individual basis. We celebrated with those whose time was up, and were sent home, but all too often they were leaving inside a "body bag," or on a stretcher with something missing.

Over the course of time many people would come, and go in one form or another. As a result, the people that made up your unit were constantly changing. Even staying in the same small unit meant you probably served with hundreds, of different people during your tour of duty. Unless you have a photographic memory, it would be difficult to remember every name, and match it with a face, but in each of our memories, certain names, and faces stood out, and for various reasons. It could have been that you were just closer friends, or it might have had something to do with what happened to them, or both. After all these years, and in talking to other Veterans, I have found that most of us can only remember somewhere between six, and twelve names. I would probably fall into this category in terms of names, but the faces have always been burned into my memory, and I can see them as vividly today, as I did then.

I have often wished I could reconnect with all those people, but wondered how such a meeting would go. Would anybody remember me after all these years? Was I a part of their memory? It's hard to say, but I have connected with a few, and one thing I noticed is that although we shared the same experience, we don't necessarily remember it in the same detail. This experience has showed me that we all deal with adversity in different ways, and some things are probably blocked out as a defense mechanism. Our recollections were as varied as our personalities.

Another problem in trying to recall the names of the people we served with was that they were given a lot of nicknames. All our Corpsmen were called "Doc." I can't tell you how many guys went by the name "Hillbilly," because of their accent. If a guy happened to be short in terms of height he would probably be called "Short Round." I can't tell you how many of each of these examples that I knew from both of my tours. One good friend of mine lost his two front teeth, and was known as "Fang." Since I was of average height, and was from the Midwest, and was told I spoke like the people on television, I didn't get an obvious nickname, instead I became known as "The Old Man." It wasn't because of my position, or age, but rather by virtue of the time that I had spent in Vietnam. Somehow, I managed to get the same nickname as Patrick, the guy that broke me in on my first tour.

One thing that seems strange to me today is that as close as we were back then, very few of us exchanged addresses so that we could get together back in the "World," but for most of us this is something that we have only recently made an attempt to do.

There were many times that I thought of trying to contact the families of those that were with me when they died. The thought of doing this probably held as much fear for me, as when I witnessed their deaths. What could you possibly say to someone that lost their son, or brother, or father? In many cases a lot of time had passed before you had the opportunity to do so, and by this time would you only make things worse for them. How would a family react to getting a phone call from a total stranger months, or even years later? I often wished that there was some kind of national directory that a family could contact, and express their desire to be contacted, or left alone, so you at least knew whether or not it would be a good idea.

I don't recall the date, but about halfway through my second tour we got a new Lieutenant. His name was John, and he was from St. Louis. He wasn't your typical new Officer. As a rule, Officers are expected to distance themselves personally from their troops. It's just part of how things work within the military structure. Our last Lieutenant had been in Vietnam for some time now, and was reassigned to a different unit to finish out his tour. It was supposed to be a gravy job. He would be flying around doing reconnaissance in a small plane. Later we heard he was shot down, and killed just before he was scheduled to go home, and John replaced him. In John's case we always knew who was in charge, but no Officer I ever saw got along so well with his men. He was respected by everyone, and there wasn't anything any of us wouldn't do for him.

At this time we had a pretty good mix of guys in the Platoon, and there was a fairly good balance of new guys, and guys with experience. Getting John rounded us off as a great Platoon to be a part of. Over the coming months we would be tested many times, and we always came through. This is not to say that we didn't have our losses, and we took each and every one very personally!

On one occasion, we had been out on an Operation, and were sent to a rear area for a couple days to regroup. This didn't happen very often, but when it did we took full advantage to try to catch up on some lost sleep. I don't think you can ever catch up, but it was nice to try after averaging about two to three hours sleep a night for months. There was also a mess hall here, which meant hot food. When we got there, the first order of business was to get something to eat. We walked over to the mess tent, grabbed a tray, and got in line. After I had my tray piled high, I went find a place to sit down, and eat. I found an opening on one of the benches, sat down, before I got one bite in my mouth, I looked up, and sitting directly across the table from me was my Cousin Ed. This was unbelievable! He had enlisted about a year after I did, and was on his first tour here. I had heard from my Mother that he was here, but what are the odds? We hung around together for the few days that we were here.

As I was getting ready to leave this, and go out on a new Operation, Ed came over to say goodbye. I told him nobody is going to believe that we ran into each other over here, and this will give us something to talk about in the future. He turned to walk away, and shouted "Hey, Look What You Talked Me Into!" In reality I didn't even know he had enlisted till he was already in, but that statement he made that day has haunted me ever since. You see, Ed was killed sometime later in Vietnam, and that was the last time I saw him alive.

There was a day coming ahead for our Platoon that would change everything for me for the rest of my life. This isn't to say that we didn't have many difficult days before with the loss of many fine young men. Just our everyday existence would have been more than most people could imagine, but one day that stood out more than any that I had ever experienced, and that was April 21st 1968. This would be the defining day that spelled out how I would live the rest of my life since then, and also the day my spirit died.

4-21-68

We had occupied a position on top of a hill several miles from Khe Sanh for several weeks. I don't remember the number of the hill, which was also it's height in elevation, and how we referred to our location. What I remember most about this hill is that we were often above the low lying clouds that surrounded it. Usually having the high ground is an advantage, as you have greater visibility. This however was not the case on most days here. Looking down all you could see were the clouds.

Our job was to maintain this position, and send small search, and destroy patrols out daily. At night we would go out, and set up ambushes, and put out listening posts. We were at Platoon strength, which consisted of three rifle squads, and a weapons squad. We were spread out in positions all around the top of the hill, and had our command post in the center. John, our Lieutenant was in command of this position, followed by our Platoon Sergeant "Dave," and then me as our Platoon Right Guide. I had been a Squad Leader up until recently, and was given this position by the Lieutenant shortly before we moved up to this hill. This position is sort of like an assistant Platoon Sergeant, and is also in charge of making sure we got the supplies we needed. Not long before we took this position, we received quite a few new replacements fresh from the states.

Sometime in the evening of 4-20-68 we received orders from Battalion Headquarters that we were to abandon this position the next morning. The next day we were going to be picked up by helicopters, and taken to Khe Sanh.

We were told that we would only be there long enough to unload our excess ammunition. From there, we were to hike out of Khe Sanh, and go up another hill to retrieve some bodies that were left from another Marine unit that had been overrun several days before.

When daylight broke on the 21st we started gathering everything up to load onto the helicopters when they arrived. Since we had occupied this position for some time now, we had quite a bit of excess ammunition. This consisted of cases of claymore mines grenades, and law rockets, and my job was to coordinate this task with the help of the three Squad Leaders. After awhile, we had a pile about three feet high, and six feet square. As this job was just about completed, the Lieutenant came out of the command post, and came over to talk to me. We talked for several minutes, and then he told me to go inside the command post, get on the radio, and find out when the helicopters were going to pick us up. On the first helicopter we would load all the excess ammunition, and then we would get on the next ones.

Within twenty seconds of my arrival inside the command post, there was a massive explosion that rocked the whole hill. Instantly, Dave, and I ran out of the bunker, and were met by a huge cloud of heavy smoke. Then we heard a lot of screaming. As the smoke started to clear, we saw a huge crater where the ammunition pile once was. We started checking with our men, and found that six had been killed, and four were severely wounded. The helicopters came shortly afterward, and we loaded our dead, and wounded on them first. Those that died never knew what hit them, and among them was John our Lieutenant. Since I didn't have a clear view, I asked some of the guys how it happened. They said we took an RPG (Rocket Propelled Grenade) round that hit the pile of ammunition. Apparently they were waiting, and watching us.

The rest of us went on to Khe Sanh. When we arrived there, we were joined up with the other Platoons in our Company. Our platoon was then ordered to lead the Company patrol to the top of the hill where the bodies from the other unit were. Since we lost our Lieutenant as well as the other men less than an hour ago, Dave became the Platoon Commander, and I became the Platoon Sergeant. At this point we had a half dozen experienced guys with us, but the rest of the Platoon consisted of new guys fresh from the states. I never even had time to learn their names, or anything about them.

It was a typical bright, and hot sunny day when we started up the hill, but all we could think about, was what had just happened to us. I'm not sure exactly how long it took to reach the summit of that hill where the bodies were. Maybe an hour, maybe it was less, but either way there wasn't much left inside of us when we got there.

The Vietnamese knew we would come back for our fallen Marines, and they were waiting. As soon as we got there they opened up on us with rockets, mortars, artillery, and machine gun fire.

Dave, along with our Platoon Corpsman "Doc Ben," would be the first ones hit. They had gotten hit by a mortar round that landed next to them. Doc Ben was killed instantly, and Dave was severely wounded. Now this left me in charge of our Platoon. I did the only thing that I could under the circumstances, and that was to try to get everybody spread out, and dug in. There were only a couple of tree stumps on top of this hill, and some craters. The rest of the hill was covered in short grass. The Vietnamese had our position zeroed in, and were lining up their shots with the tree stumps and adjusting their rounds accordingly. I was taking two guys at a time with me, and running to various places on the hill to get them spread out, and dug in. I turned around and saw the last two get hit, but the others were catching even more hell where they were at, so I had to move them, and get them spread out, and dug in. There was no safe place to run.

Sometime during the time I was running, I saw a mortar round land in front of me. It blew me off my feet, and I landed on the back of my head. Fortunately, I had only sustained some minor shrapnel wounds, but got my ear drums blown out, and got a concussion. Eventually I ended up in a hole with two other men, one being my radio operator "Willy," and a new squad leader named "Louie," along with the bodies, and parts of bodies lost by that other unit a few days ago. Since we were under constant fire, we couldn't get any helicopters to come in, and pick up the wounded. We would be here all night under fire. One thing that made this particularly difficult for me was that the new guys only knew my name, and called out all night for me to help them. Once during the night the Vietnamese made an attempt to overrun us, but we threw a few grenades down the hill, and they stopped.

Since the rest of the company was also catching hell there

was nobody to call for help, and we were pretty much on our own. The Company Gunnery Sergeant called me on the radio, and said "hang in there kid we're doing all that we can do for you." We called in for air strikes early on, but they weren't effective in stopping the pounding we were taking.

Somewhere around nine the next morning it stopped as suddenly as it started. We got helicopters to come in, but by this time there was only one man in our whole platoon that didn't get killed or at least wounded either on the first hill, or this one.

This was only one 24 hour period of time out of the 25 months that I spent in Vietnam, but this was the last day I spent in Combat. It is something I have thought about everyday of my life since then, and been forced to relive through nightmares over, and over again. One of my greatest frustrations over the years is that I can't remember all the names of the faces that live within me.

For those of us that were able, we loaded the wounded on the first helicopters according to the severity of their wounds. This was determined by one of the Corpsman "Doc Ski," who came over from the 3rd Platoon to help us out, since our Corpsman had been killed. After this was accomplished, we loaded the ones from our Platoon that had been killed, and the ones from the other unit that had been killed several days before. Then the rest of us boarded for a quick flight to the hospital. Once we got to the hospital, some of us were first taken to the morgue, which was really just a tent where they processed the necessary information. They wanted us to try to identify those that were killed from our Platoon, but the other ones were there as well. Once we did this, we went back over to the hospital, and received treatment for our wounds. I had one piece of shrapnel removed from my knee, one from the side of my head, and one from my hand. There were still a few more pieces in me including one that was very close to my right eye. For this I had to go see an eye Doctor. Eventually he determined that it wouldn't cause any problem to my sight, and decided to leave it in.

I was twenty years old at this time, but I looked like I was twice that and more. I think there is a breaking point for all of us, and maybe through the course of our lives we will come to find what that is for us as individuals. Sometime while I was in the hospital, I found mine. I can only describe it as a complete mental meltdown. I don't recall all of the details of it, because most of it is still just a big blur to me, but I have since been told by other people what had happened. A couple buddies (Fergie and Fang) came to see me in the hospital, and said they couldn't believe how I looked. They said my eyes were as big as silver dollars, and I couldn't talk, but I don't remember them being there. It started with a local Vietnamese person that worked in the hospital doing mainly cleanup jobs. He walked past the bed I was in, carrying a broom, and they tell me I jumped up, and grabbed him, and threw him to the ground, and attempted to strangle him. Then a bunch of the medical staff tried to restrain me, and I fought them as well. They eventually won, and strapped me down to a stretcher, and gave me a shot of something. The next thing I remember was waking up on a bus still strapped down, in New Jersey! I had been sent home, and was initially taken to Fort Dix Army Hospital, but only stayed there one long night. I couldn't sleep, I couldn't talk, and I couldn't move, but there was a Nurse on the night shift that just stayed by me, and talked to me. I have no idea who she was, or what she said at the time, but her voice was soothing, and it helped me relax a little bit.

The next morning I was transferred to Philadelphia Naval Hospital, and was placed in their Psychiatric Unit. This would be home for me for the next couple months.

Chapter 10

Some Wounds Don't Bleed

They didn't have a name for the problems I had at this time. Years later they would call this post traumatic stress disorder, or PTSD, and found that many guys had experienced this on varying levels. It can manifest itself in a number of ways, but generally you feel angry, or depressed to the point where you cannot function. It also comes with a strong feeling of guilt, and frustration, accompanied by intrusive thoughts, or flashbacks, and nightmares. You find yourself unable to concentrate on anything, but your war experience. You can only sleep with medication, and thoughts of suicide are always with you. With proper treatment, some people manage to learn to cope with everyday life, but for many of us, this will become a lifetime sentence.

During the time I spent in Philadelphia, treatment for all practical purposes, was nonexistent. The only thing they did here was load you up with drugs. My days consisted of sitting around one large open ward with approximately thirty other guys that were here for all types of problems, and not necessarily combat related. For example, there was one guy here that had murdered his wife, and was being evaluated. In the mornings the Doctors would walk around to each man, and ask him how he felt that day, and wrote down whatever his response was. That was the total extent of treatment offered at this time. Every so often, the Doctor would tell me he would send me home with a medical discharge and a disability if I were agreeable to that. If you left, you were no longer their problem. They really pushed for this, because the place was crowded, and they needed the space, and besides they didn't know what to do with you anyway.

The ward was always locked, and when you came here they took away everything that they thought you might hurt yourself with, or somebody else. I had a small picture with me, but they took the frame, along with my shoelaces. Once a day they passed out razors to shave, but they had a special locking device in them so that you couldn't remove the blade. They closely monitored us here, and everywhere else for that matter. The only other place we could go was an adjacent outside area that had a twelve foot fence around it, with rolls of barbed wire at the top. In reality, the only difference between being here, and being in prison, was here they gave you drugs. In prison you would have to find a source.

When I first got here, my family including Patty flew here to see me. They would allow visitors, but they were also closely monitored. I only spent a couple hours with them, and ironically they thought I looked pretty good. They were looking to see what the wounds had done to me. What they couldn't see were the wounds inside me. These are the ones that don't bleed.

Problems like these, over the years since then are treated in a different manner. When catastrophic events occur now, they have "Crisis Intervention Teams" to take care of those involved. This however, still isn't in place the way it should be for those returning from a war zone. Somehow we always manage to treat returning Veterans with less compassion. We as a country still suffer from both short-term memory loss, as well as long-term memory loss. We ask our young people to fight for their country, but when they come back with some problems as a result of it, we generally ignore them. The treatment for those of us during Vietnam left a lot to be desired. Our society wanted us out of sight, and out of mind. We were and still are a society that wants everything handled in a fast-food manner, and are unwilling to take the time to do it right. Today the attitude toward our Veterans isn't as bad as it was then, but as time goes by, will we maintain the patience, and perseverance to take care of our Veterans whose problems won't go away the minute the war is over? For many of the returning Vietnam Veterans, the wounds they received by coming home, were worse than the ones they received in combat. There may come a day where the very existence of this country will be at stake, and if we keep treating our Veterans in this manner, there may not be anyone willing to step up, and defend it. Any country that doesn't take care of its Veterans, is morally bankrupt, and will eventually cease to exist.

There still doesn't seem to be a cure for what I have, although there are some methods of treatment. While in the hospital in Philadelphia, I had to learn how to fight a new battle, and that was one of survival. I had to pretend that everything was just fine, and that there was absolutely nothing wrong with me. I thought that if no one wanted to hear about my problems, that I would just deny that I had any. So that's what I told the Doctors, and they eventually released me back to duty. I would spend the rest of my life playing a role, as if I were a movie star. Instead of living a life, I chose an existence that I had to carefully control. Over the years, I perfected to the point where I later told my wife that I should have won an Oscar. For a time I had even convinced myself, but the reality of how I really felt was always there, and that I couldn't control. I would get nightly reminders in the form of Nightmares, and my thoughts during the day were more of the same.

I had about a year left on my enlistment when I left Philadelphia. This time I was given orders to report to Camp Lejeune, North Carolina. I was assigned to another Grunt unit, only this time I would be "playing war" in the woods of North Carolina, and many of the men had also just returned from Vietnam. I wasn't there very long before they told us we would be going to Cuba for six months. It was difficult enough playing war in North Carolina, but I really wasn't up to going to Cuba. So, I managed to get myself transferred to the Base Security Company, and once I got there, they told me I would be going to the Headquarters of the Marine Corps in Washington D.C. to work on an Officers Promotion Board.

Going to D.C. was considered a temporary duty assignment lasting a few months. Since my enlistment would be up while I was there, they told me to take everything with me. The only way I would possibly go back to Camp Lejeune was if I reenlisted. When I got there, I was put up in a barracks with mostly guys awaiting orders, or getting discharged. The Board that I worked on consisted of one other enlisted man that was a Sergeant, and the rest were Officers, and most of them were Majors, and Lt. Colonels. The work was kind of interesting, but a little bit tedious. I was treated well, considering I was the lowest ranking person there. One thing that made the job difficult was the Board room where we worked, overlooked Arlington Cemetery. Almost everyday there was a funeral in progress outside our windows. This brought back a lot of memories of when I had to participate in these in San Francisco. This always left me feeling depressed. I had a desk job, but it seemed that no matter where I went, death was following me. Most of the time I spent here, and even when I wasn't working, I just stared out into the thousand of rows of white crosses.

As the board was nearing an end, they started pressuring me about reenlistment. This is what I had always dreamed about, and planned to do ever since I was a little kid, but now I was torn between running away, and never leaving. They sent me to see a career counselor. He just went over all the options that I would have if I decided to stay in. At the time, they would give you another stripe, a choice of where you wanted to be stationed for two years, a cash bonus, and in some cases a change in your M.O.S., or job specialty. After he spelled this all out, he asked me what I planned to do. I told him that I wasn't sure, and that's what he wrote down on my paperwork. I guess I thought I would keep my options open. I would get out for awhile, but I could always go back in, if things didn't work out for me on the outside. Besides, maybe all I needed was some time to get my head on straight.

When my last day arrived, I was more nervous, than when I had enlisted. I had to go through the check out procedure, which took about two hours to complete. Then I was just standing there with all my possessions in two bags, and with my paperwork completed in my hand. I walked toward the gate to leave the base for the last time, but when I got there, I just stopped for awhile, and stared at it. It may have only been a couple minutes, but it seemed like I stood there for hours. Then I walked out. I couldn't believe that I had done this. What the hell was wrong with me! This is not how my life was supposed to go. Most guys were happy when they got out, and celebrated, and in some cases for days, or weeks, or even longer. All I felt was a sense of failure.

Going home brought on a whole new set of challenges. When you are experiencing an emotional problem that everybody around you is aware of, you get the sense that they are watching you, and every move you make. So, in addition to whatever problems you may have already had, a feeling of paranoia overcomes you. The fact is that you already felt like you didn't have anything in common with the people around you, and were unable to discuss it with them either. You felt like you couldn't trust anyone, and it didn't matter what your relationship had been with them before. Hell, you felt like you couldn't trust yourself! It was your problem, not theirs. The way in which society treats people with these types of problems is far different, than with any other type of medical issue. You didn't fit in, and you lost you capacity to trust others, and as a result made the people around you uncomfortable as well. Neither of us knew what to say to each other. So you see there is paranoia on both sides of these problems.

There are some things that I had learned from the Marine Corps that are still a part of me today, and would kick in whenever I was placed in a difficult situation. The discipline that was beaten into us from the day we arrived in boot camp probably kept me alive. It was reliable, and it was automatic. Just do what you had to do, and survive!

I had applied for a job on our local Police Department, and when I took the entrance examination I came out on the top of the list. I was hired, and went off to the Police Academy. I graduated, and was President of the class, voted "Most likely to succeed." On the first day I reported for work, one of the guys thought he would give the rookie a little harassment. He was trying to tease me by saying "wait till you go on a call, and see your first dead one." I wanted to beat the crap out of him, but the discipline kicked in, and I just stood there, and took it. Another guy had been watching this, and knew that I had been in Vietnam, and told him that I probably had seen things that he wouldn't see in an entire career. That guy had served in Korea. I ended up hating this job, but really didn't know why at the time. I quit six months later. In retrospect, this was probably a good thing, because it was not a good time for me to be carrying a gun.

The one bright spot for me was when Patty and I got married. For some reason she, and I fit together perfectly, and this was despite the problems I had come home with. We could always rely upon each other, and no matter what we faced together, or individually, we supported each other through it. Things have not always been easy for us, but we're still standing, and she is the reason that I'm alive today.

Chapter 11

The '70s

Vietnam was still going on, but now my view of it was watching it unfold on television. For me, being a spectator, instead of a participant seemed strange. I felt on more than one occasion that I wanted to go back again. Somehow in my mind I felt that I was needed there, or maybe by going back I could change the outcome of my experience.

Anyway, it was always right there in front of me, and would remain so for many years to come.

You really didn't have to watch the news to hear Vietnam mentioned. Now there were Movies being made about it, and there were even characters on television shows that were portraying Vietnam Veterans. There was one universal theme used in the making of these movies, television shows, and that was the makeup of what the typical Veteran was like. They usually had Vietnam Veterans fit into a certain type of criteria. They were Psychotic, Drug-addicted, Alcoholic, Homeless, Jobless, and couldn't hold onto a Relationship. If you voiced any opposition to these portrayals you were considered a crybaby. I have often wondered how the World War II Veterans would have felt, if this is how they were portrayed after the war.

Sometime during these years the "News Media" changed their own job description. Telling us about an event that had just occurred was no longer the priority, and was replaced by giving us their "opinion" of the event. They just seemed to be caught up in their own celebrity. They even coined a name for one of the news anchors as "The Most Trusted Man in America." If he was just reporting the facts of the story alone, then why should we have to worry about our trust in him? Maybe they meant that all the others were lying to the general public. When this man "reported" that the Vietnam War could no longer be won, the Politicians, as well as the country bought it. This was in reference to the "Tet Offensive" of 1968. The facts were that yes, the enemy launched a major offensive throughout the country, but they lost every battle by a large margin. If this type of reporting had been done in World War II, I suppose we should have surrendered to Germany, and Japan.

Most Americans aligned themselves with one or another of these "Celebrity" newscasters, and when they spoke, it was gospel. You cannot underestimate the influence these people had on the country. Just as most Politicians caved into the pressure of the media, the Veterans themselves started believing what was being said about them. If everywhere you turned, people were telling you that you cannot, and will not succeed in life, as a result of your war experience you are then left with two choices. One is to live the way they made you out to be, and the other is to prove them wrong. Both of these paths were followed in one way, or another by most Veterans. Some had developed drinking problems, or drug problems as a result of the bombardment they had received in combat, while many others developed these habits to numb themselves to the hostile environment they received when they came home. Other Veterans were over-achievers, but usually at the cost of being a workaholic.

Trust like respect, is something you have to earn. It should not be given solely on the basis of position or title. In this era we seemed to forget this. We assumed what we were being told was accurate, and trusted some individuals to tell us the truth. It had become an easy way to take in the world around you. Here was a person in your living room every night telling you what was going on, and you didn't even have to take the time to read about it. On the surface, this seems like a very efficient method to keeping informed, after all, your life was busy enough, and you had better things to do with your time. The media seemed to be of the opinion that either the American Public was either stupid and had to be given their "expert opinion," or couldn't be trusted with the truth. The only problem with this is that you lost your ability think independently. Over the years since, the truth has become even more blurred. The "Celebrity News Media" of today is even more money driven, then they were during this time. They are competing for your audience based upon ratings that translate into money. It's not the accuracy of the news, or which station scooped the others on a breaking story that determines this either. Today it's more related to the appearance of telling the truth, and the appearance in physical terms of the newscaster, and probably in equal proportions. At any rate, during the Vietnam War the media contributed, and perpetuated the stereotypical images of what happened in Vietnam, and more importantly, the negative image of the Veteran that fought there.

Ironically, in the 25 months that I spent in Vietnam, I only saw one newsperson, and he was a freelance photojournalist. While he was with me he got wounded himself, and received a telegram from "The Most Trusted Man in America" in the hospital.

After I left the Police Department, I got a job driving a truck through my Uncle. It served the purpose of making a paycheck, and I definitely need that. Patty had gotten pregnant three weeks after we were married, and now I was going to have to support a wife and a child in the near future. She asked me if I wanted a boy, or a girl, despite the popular opinion that all men wanted sons, I told her that I wanted a daughter, because I couldn't bare the idea of a son going off to war sometime in the future. On May 18 1970 we welcomed our daughter "Kelly" into the world, and on March 3 1974 we welcomed our daughter "Kerry" into the world. This would be as many children as we would have. Ironically, by the time my daughters reached the age where young men could be sent to war, girls were now taking combat roles in the military.

I had a fairly large extended family. In 1947, the year in which I was born, I had six cousins also born that same year. There were three girls, and four boys counting myself. Of the four boys, three of us went to Vietnam, and all were in the Marine Corps.
I was the first to go and the other two went a year, or so later. My cousin Ed was killed in Vietnam in October of 1970. Later his younger brother also went into the Marine Corps.
When Ed died people outside of the family weren't particularly kind to his Mother concerning the loss of her son. The implications being that he had it coming for his participation in this war, or what did you expect anyway? Very few families received the compassion they deserved when their loved one was lost. My other cousin "Rich" also went to Vietnam, didn't get wounded, but had some problems over the years since, and basically disappeared from the rest of the family. The fourth boy that was born that year in our family went to Canada to avoid the draft, and later told me that myself, as well as the others would be going to hell for what we had done over there.
There were many times during the 70s that I wanted to go back in the Marine Corps. My wife, and I talked about it many

times, and she would have supported me if I had done that. I just never felt like I fit into this new world I came home to. There was a constant feeling of wanting to run away, but not knowing where to go. I even thought of leaving the country many times, because I felt that this country didn't want us, and I didn't want to live in a country that felt that way. As individuals we may have changed, but we also came home to a changed country.

Earlier on, I said that I was part of the crowd during high school that planned to go in the service after graduation. The majority of these guys died in Vietnam, So, I lost a lot of friends at home as well. There were eighteen guys that got killed from my hometown, and the majority of them were my friends in high school. So, when I came home there weren't too many of my old friends to hang around with, and I dam sure didn't have anything in common with my other contemporaries.

All through the 70s it seemed as though the country was mad about the war. The implication, or should I say indictment of the Vietnam Veteran was that they somehow were responsible for the war itself, and sometimes it came from sources that you wouldn't expect. Older generations of Veterans sometimes implied that we had let the country down. Regardless of what the majority of Veterans did, they were all painted with the same brush. Just by being a Veteran of this era, you were considered a lost soul of society, and incapable of doing anything meaningful with your life. Nothing heroic was ever portrayed, or reported, at least not without the usual characterizations. No other group of Veterans from any previous war had ever been treated in this manner by their country, and its citizens. So, when so little is expected from you, it isn't difficult to live down to these expectations.

I applied for a job, and had to go before a review board of commissioners for an oral interview. The man in charge of this board was well known in the community, and was the Post Commander of the largest local Veterans Service Organization. At the time, I thought that this would be favorable to me, since I was a Veteran. When I sat down I felt somewhat confident in my chances of getting the job, plus there was supposed to be a law that gave you preference toward the job. After the first comment, made by the president of the board I knew this would not be the case. He said, "I see by your application that you are a Vietnam Veteran." "How much dope did you smoke while you were there?" He then rambled on about how we as a group of Veterans were a bunch of crybabies, and that we didn't fight in a real war like him, and his buddies. I couldn't believe what this man was saying at the time, and just sat there dumbfounded, and took it. This should have come as no surprise to me, considering everything else people were saying at the time, but here was a man that was a Veteran himself talking this way. Needless to say, my confidence quickly turned to a resignation that I wouldn't be getting this job. When I left, they told me that if I didn't hear from them in three weeks that I should assume that I wouldn't be put on their hiring list. So, three weeks, four weeks, five weeks rolled by, and I never heard from them.

About a year, and a half later, my wife called me where I was working at the time, and said that the place I had that oral interview with called, and wanted to talk to me. So, I called them back to see what they wanted. The man on the phone said, "Hey asshole, you want a job?" I told him he must be looking for somebody else, because I wasn't on their list. Then he said that he had the list right in front of him, and my name was the next one up. Well, I was never told that I made the list, and consequently wasn't allowed to use my military preference points. They can only be used when the list comes out, and then after that, you can use them to move yourself further up the list. Not one other guy that made this list was a Veteran, but there were several that took this test besides me. I found out later that had if I been allowed to use those points that I would have been first on that list.

I was disgusted by the treatment I had received from these people, and told my wife what had happened. She begged me not to take the job, and told me I deserved better than this. She asked me what I was going to do, and as much as I didn't want to, I took the job anyway. I needed a job, and this one paid fairly well, but I would never feel any satisfaction from working there. I also never took a promotional exam while I worked there. This was for two reasons, the first being that I would have to go before the same board that hired me, and the second was because of my last day in Vietnam. I swore that I never wanted to be in charge of anyone else ever again. I did what I had to do, not what I wanted to do, and felt a great loss of self-respect.

For the next 25 years I would literally work around the clock. I held as many as three jobs at one time. On an average week I would put in between 100, and 120 hours a week between them. This seemed like a solution to help me forget about Vietnam. If I was busy enough, then maybe I wouldn't have enough time to think about it. There was only one time that I couldn't escape those thoughts, and that was at night. I would attempt to go to sleep, and just lay there restless for hours, and eventually pass out. Then I would wake every hour on the hour usually as a result of nightmares. I would get up, and walk around the house looking for an unseen enemy. The content of these nightmares were pretty much the same every night. Usually it consisted of a vivid recollection of my war experiences, or one where I felt hands trying to pull me into a grave, and in both cases I heard their voices, and saw their faces. Even during the day I was always worried that people were looking at me, and I was always afraid that that if somehow I appeared differently to them, they would lock me up, and throw away the key. So I did whatever I could to not call attention to myself or allow people to get too close, and if this was unavoidable, then I did my absolute best to pretend that I was the most normal person they had ever met.

There was one thought that entered our minds from time to time while in Vietnam, and that was the thought of being captured. Personally I thought that if we were captured, they would just kill us, and possibly torture us first. The vast majority of POWs were Pilots that had been shot down over Vietnam, and they were all Officers. As an enlisted man, and a Grunt at that, we figured we weren't much of a trophy for them to keep us alive, so our chance of survival, if captured, didn't seem like much of a possibility. The one thing that was, and is universal among Vietnam Veterans is how we felt for all our POWs. We held each and every man that was missing, or captured close to our hearts. It was one area where we as a group would not compromise. We wanted them back with no exceptions! In 1973, the North Vietnamese began releasing our POWs. We watched those frail, but honorable men return back to us, and were filled with unbelievable emotions. Perhaps part of this that isn't obvious to everyone else is that it represented a Victory to us, and something to celebrate for once.

I don't know if there are any POWs still being held captive as some people contend, but even if there isn't, we should hold a special place in our hearts for them, because some of them died as a result of their treatment, or lack of it. I'm glad to see the POW/MIA flags flown, because it offers a fitting tribute to these men.

In April of 1975 we quietly left Vietnam. Although some people may have felt like celebrating the end of our involvement in Vietnam, for most of us this would be a time spent in hollow reflection, and isolation. It's not that we wanted the war to continue, and we certainly didn't want any more lives lost, but the fact that we just left in the manner offered no conclusion for us. As a result, the war would never be over for us individually, and since that was the way most of us came home, we were left to deal with it on our own. There was no recognition on a personal level, or as part of a group for what we had been through. There was no honor given, no respect, and if anything, we were treated with contempt. We were made to feel as though somehow we were responsible for the war, and that we shamed the country by losing it. In the first place, we didn't lose the war, or create it. Our country and its leaders just decided to pull the plug on it. As an example, this would be like being in the deciding game of the World Series with a ten run lead, and then walking off the field in forfeiture. In all the time we spent there, we never lost one major battle. Yes, just like in every other war, many young lives were lost. The war was lost here, in this country, not by the Veterans, but by the country itself for not having the will to win. I won't try to justify the merits of our choosing to fight in Vietnam in the first place. This was a decision by the leaders of this government who were elected by a majority of Americans. The only thing that Veterans were guilty of was fighting in your name. The rules of war are remarkably simple. You do whatever is necessary to end it quickly, and efficiently, and with the minimum loss of life that is humanly possible, but you must win! If you feel that any one of these rules cannot be complied with, then you've already lost. Once you're already there, it is too late to be discussing whether or not you should be. The only thing accomplished by this, is to pull the rug out from underneath the troops you sent there. War is not an ideal, a concept, a belief, nor a perception, but rather a brutal action taken by man based upon these thoughts.

Chapter 12

The '80s

I don't know how, or why, but sometime during the 80s it suddenly became fashionable to be a Vietnam Veteran. Maybe enough years had passed since then, or maybe the country was finally willing to begin to deal with it. On the surface this would seem like a good thing, but the country's sudden fascination was largely based upon the mythical characterizations of just what a Veteran was supposed to be like. More movies had been made depicting the same old stereotypes, and rather take an insightful look into the reality, people just made assumptions. It wasn't uncommon in the 80s for guys that had never been in the service, let alone in Vietnam, to try to pass themselves off as Vietnam Veterans in social situations, by posing as a Vietnam Veteran just for the reaction they got. All they had to do was memorize a few lines from the latest movie, and use them in a bar. There were even some that used this ploy at work. I guess they derived some sick satisfaction from being able to tell people how misunderstood they were, and that nobody had better mess with them, because they would do just what they saw the guy in the movie do. So, now our stereotypical image was being acted out by imposters.

Some groups of Veterans encouraged the politicians in Chicago to have a "Welcome Home Parade" for Vietnam Veterans. The concept was very well received, and a day for the parade was set aside. Some people asked me if I was going to go, but I had mixed feelings about it. On one hand it seemed like some better late than never recognition for the Veterans as a group, but on the other hand, I felt that since the idea originated with the Veterans themselves, that there wasn't much joy in throwing yourself a parade, and nearly twenty years after the fact. It turned out that the whole community had gotten behind it, and there was some real support after all. I didn't attend the parade, even though I lived there. In retrospect, I regret not having gone to it, because some years later I talked to some guys that had been there, and they told me how good it made them feel. I probably also lost out on a potential chance of finding somebody that served with me in Vietnam.

During this time the "Vietnam Wall" was unveiled in Washington. Once again it took the Veterans themselves to get the project off the ground. When the plans were first announced that they were going to build a memorial to those that died in Vietnam, I felt overwhelmed, and grateful. There were many ideas given about how it should look. It was then decided that a competition would be held to determine whose design entry would be used.

One of the design characteristics for the memorial was to have everyone's name that had died in Vietnam engraved on it. This seemed like a great idea to me, and for this alone I will be eternally grateful. My opinion wasn't the same for the rest of the concept. I had been stationed in Washington at the end of my enlistment, and was familiar with how the city looked. The first thing that stood out was the black granite surface of the memorial. Washington is a sea of towering white marble memorials. My initial impression was this one looked as though it was deliberately made to look like a black mark on our piece of history. Then I thought that maybe this would help call greater attention to it, by being different, and maybe that wouldn't be so bad. Later I found out it was going to be recessed into the ground so that you were literally walking downhill, and below the surrounding land to view it. You could actually drive right by it, and never even know it was there, and be less than a hundred yards away from it. I know there are countless numbers of people that find this design extremely moving, and a fitting tribute to the men, and women listed on its surface, and I may be the only one that feels this way, but to me it just doesn't represent the people whose names are engraved on it in a way I would have expected. I know many names on that wall, and it is only by the grace of God that my name isn't among them. Over the years since it was built, it has become the most visited memorial in Washington. Some people claim they feel a sense of healing in going there, but I just don't get the same feeling.

In July of 1982 the man that I had admired most, and used to measure myself by, died suddenly. He was my Father, and I don't think I ever got over the loss. He was 62 years old at the time. I could always turn to him when I had any problems. Just being around him made me feel good, and I have to say that anyone that knew him also felt that way. Now I felt more alone than ever, and there was no one else that could fill that void. As a man you gage yourself by the men that you see around you as you're growing up, and the influence they have whether good, or bad has a lot to do with who you become. I never realized how much I relied upon him even into my adult life.

On Christmas Eve 1985 my Mother suffered a heart attack. She survived it, and was released from the hospital on January 4 1986. Later that same day she had another heart attack, and was taken back to the hospital where she died immediately after she arrived. Personally I think she died of a broken heart in July 1982. She was 64 years old. My parents had been married for over forty years, and I don't think either one of them could imagine living without the other. My Mother was a woman that would cry when you cried, and rejoice with you when you were happy, and was always concerned about the welfare of others before her own. As Parents I had been given very much, and it isn't until something like this happens that you fully understand what you lost. I wish I still had them around. I miss them very much.

Even though I had a great relationship with my parents, and had the complete support of my wife, when it came to the subject of Vietnam, I never discussed anything about how I really felt. It's not that the subject never came up, but I couldn't tell anyone, including them. I never told them about all the things that tortured my mind. For one thing, as I said earlier, I had been trying to cover it up ever since I came back. My whole life to this point was an act. I had gotten so good at pretending, that my mother told me one time that she was so glad that she never had to worry about me, outside of the time I was in Vietnam. She meant this as a complement, but she had no idea just how screwed up I was.

There was a Senator that made a run for the Presidency during this time, and when it was found out that he earlier sought treatment for depression, he had to drop out of the race. This incident only served to reaffirm my belief that in our society this type of illness is unacceptable. We tell people there is help out there for them, but if they seek it out, they become labeled. As far as I can see, the stigma is still there. What people say, and how they really feel about it are two completely different things. Ask yourself how you would be treated by your friends, relatives, and co-workers if you made them aware that you were suffering with this kind of problem. When someone commits suicide, we just say that they were mentally ill. I personally believe many of the attempts that people make aren't part of the illness, but are done out of the shame they feel for having this type of problem in the first place. The fear people feel concerning how they will be perceived with this type of illness is probably the only thought that they have that isn't irrational.

During the latter part of the '80s I began to feel a strong need to try to reconnect with some of the guys that I served with. This would be a difficult undertaking, since many years had passed, and I was relying on a clouded memory. I had none of their addresses, and could only remember a few of their full names. Then many of them had nicknames back in those days, and that's all you knew them by. I wondered if they would even want to get reacquainted. Would I be digging up painful memories for them? Would their lives have mirrored mine? As much as I wanted to talk to them again, the fear of such an encounter weighed heavy on my mind. I did always talk about one guy to my wife, and I even had an old picture of us together. I knew he lived in Florida, and I knew the town, but I didn't do anything about it. Then one day my wife told me that she put an ad in the local news paper where he lived without telling me as a surprise. The guys Mother saw the ad, and told him about it, and he called me. I was thrilled, but nervous, and figured he was too. We talked several more times, and then I told him I would fly to Florida to see him, and we made arrangements to visit together.

My heart was pounding when I boarded the plane for Florida. Even though we had talked several times on the phone, I was still unsure what it was going to be like seeing each other face to face for the first time in all these years. In fact this was to be the first time I saw anyone that I served with, since I left that hill in Vietnam. He was one of the two guys that spent the whole night with me in that hole in the ground the last night I was in combat. When the plane landed I looked around to find a familiar face. There was none to be seen. I guess I assumed he would be standing there waiting for me. In the nervous conversations we had on the phone this was never made clear. So, I rented a car and drove about an hour to where he lived. When I got there I knocked on the door, but no one answered. I was really getting nervous, but I kept telling myself he must have had some problem that I was unaware of, and that it had nothing to do with me. I drove around for awhile and came back, and still no answer. My wife, and I decided to just wait there for awhile, and he would probably be pulling up any minute. After about an hour we went to get something to eat, and came back again. This time I knocked on the door, and it swung open real fast, and he looked like I startled him. We went in, but you could cut the tension with a knife. After an hour or so we left, and went to check into a motel, and went back the next day like we had discussed with him, but the atmosphere wasn't much better. When we left, I told him we should keep in touch, and he nodded his head that he would and we left. That was the last contact with him I have had. I have tried to call many times, but never got an answer, and then later his phone was disconnected. I was closer to this man at one time than I had been with anyone else. Maybe his problems were worse than mine.

Several people had told me that they announced on the Oprah Winfrey Show that they were looking for Vietnam Veterans to be in their audience to review a movie that had been made about Vietnam, and that I should go. At first I dismissed the idea, because of the way I felt about how the movies had exploited the Veterans, then I thought about the parade that I didn't attend, so I decided I would go. I went to the show, and got a seat in the front row. I don't know what I was thinking, because if I couldn't communicate how I felt to my own family, how was I going to do it on camera to the rest of the world? I just sat there through the whole show, and couldn't say a word. There was something that I did take away from that show. A seed of inspiration was planted to find another way to communicate how I felt to other people, and what you are reading now, is the form that it took, although it has taken nearly twenty years to get started. The thought of putting it down on paper would have never occurred to me without that experience I had that day.

In 1989 I moved from my hometown. I had always felt the need to go somewhere else, and this partly because I thought some new surroundings would somehow change my life. It was though I thought I could start my life over again, if I moved to a new area. Outside of the time I spent in the service, I lived here my whole life, and felt the need for a change. I ended up moving only thirty miles away, but at least there were new surroundings. Not long after I moved, I quit working all the extra jobs, and only worked one for a change. I didn't miss working the other jobs, but now I had too much time to think again. Inevitably my thoughts went back to Vietnam. I ended up unable to sleep very much, which in turn gave me even more time to think about it. I was right back to where it was before, only now it was even more frequent. My wife would plead for me to get involved in other things, but I wouldn't listen, and really just didn't want to leave the house. I wasn't happy at work, but always put up a good front there. I never complained about my job or anything else for that matter to my wife. There was absolutely no one I felt that I could trust outside of my home. I used to tell my wife that if you expect the worst from people, you'll never be disappointed! That is how I saw life, and how I chose to live it.

Chapter 13

The '90s

The early '90s began with yet another war. This time, like most people I would watch it from my living room. I couldn't keep my eyes off of it, and watched it around the clock. You could easily say I was obsessed with watching the reports come in. While it was going on, I couldn't think about much else. I was drawn into it as though I was there myself. In terms of how it was being carried out, the Gulf War was very different than what my experience had been. Ironically, shortly before it began, I looked into going into the Military Reserves. I had even picked up the necessary paperwork, and had discussed it with my wife, and was very interested in doing it. There was still a strong attachment to the military for me, and maybe this would serve to fill the void. This was just before I moved, and I put it on hold for the time being, because I wanted to get settled into the new house first. If I had followed through with it, the unit I was planning on joining was one of the first reserve units sent to the Gulf. This was a foreign concept to me, because when I was in the service, reserve units with very few exceptions were never sent overseas. In fact, many guys went in them to fulfill their military obligation, and not be sent to Vietnam. Back then they were called "Weekend Warriors," and they reported one weekend a month, and went to what they called summer camp for two weeks during the summer. When I was in North Carolina we had to train them and didn't think very highly of them, because we felt they had taken the easy way out. Nowadays they seem like they're almost the first to go, and I wonder if we keep using them in this fashion how many guys will continue to join?

The word "Draft" during Vietnam was considered a four letter word. Given the fact that we have to maintain a certain level of military strength I wonder how many times we are going to supplement this strength with our reserve units before there is no one left standing there. They want an all volunteer Army, but what happens if you drive the men, and women out of the reserves, by over using them? Will we have enough active duty people to make up the loss, or is the much dreaded four letter word going to have to make another reappearance? I personally don't have a problem with the Draft, except for one huge exception, and that is that there can be no deferments, with the exception of real medical issues! During Vietnam we granted deferments for those that went to college. So in this land of equal opportunity, we placed a far greater value on those people that had the ability, and money to go to college.

The Gulf War didn't last very long, but it did serve to rekindle, and reinforce the intrusive thoughts that were always a part of my life. The numbers of lives lost by our country were few in comparison to Vietnam, but one is too much to take if you're the family that receives the telegram. For those families there is no amount of consolation that will lessen their loss. For some of those brave young men, and women that were participants, the war will never be over. War doesn't end just because they say it's over, and they sent you home. There is no set amount of time, or length of experience that it takes to have a profound affect on your life. Talk about it every chance you get. Today people are willing to listen, and if you need help, by all means seek it out. Stay in touch with those you served with. Even if you're doing fine, there may be one of your comrades out there that could use a little support. Remember, you and your comrades are the only ones that know what you went through.

Maybe because I was pre-conditioned to these feelings, but now some of my nightmares include the Gulf War, and I wasn't even there. Just seeing the daily reports on television made me feel that I was somehow involved. In a way I felt that I should have been there. When War is such a big part of your life, you always feel that even though you may have had too much of it, you keep going back to what you know. Maybe you think you can somehow change the outcome, or maybe you think your life has passed you by, or maybe it's the rush you get from the intensity of it. All of my adult life was spent feeling guilty for surviving, not that I had a death wish or something like that, but there were times that I felt that this was the only alternative that I had to escape the pain that I was feeling. As a result, a good part of the time I felt physically, and emotionally exhausted.

I started taking up fishing for recreational purposes. There is a sense of solace that you feel being out on the water that you don't find in many other places. I couldn't escape the thoughts I had even here, but the calming effect of being on the water helped me relax. You could reflect on your past, but in a much calmer way. I spent many hours by myself doing just that. To me it didn't matter if I caught a fish, or not. It was just the atmosphere it provided me with. I think I found a means of therapy that actually works. I saw a sign in a bait shop that read "For every hour you spend fishing, you add a day back into your life," and I believe it to be true.

On July 31 1996 I became a Grandpa for the first time and two more times since then, and I just found out that there is another one on the way. So far they're all boys, but it's too early to tell with the most recent one. Grandkids are better than kids, (only kidding girls).

In the late 90s I went to get an annual physical for work. The Doctor didn't like what he saw, and sent me for some additional testing. I had to go see a Cardiologist, and have a stress test. He didn't like the results and felt I needed an angiogram. The results showed a blockage, so an angioplasty was scheduled. The only other time I had been in a hospital was for encephalitis in the summer of 1976. That time I was there for three weeks, with the first week in isolation to determine if it was the contagious type. I had to have a lot of spinal taps with that one. This time they did an angioplasty, and placed a stent in the artery to open the blockage.

Since having that procedure I was put on a bunch of prescriptions, and now I have to take the contents of a small drugstore everyday, but I'm still kicking.

Chapter 14

The Turn of the Century

There was a lot of hype about the calendar turning over to 2000. People were preoccupied with a sort of impending doom, because there were a lot of stories circulating that all our computers would suddenly go blank. This of course did not happen, but it was a hot story for awhile. The millennium rang in pretty much like any other year.

This was the year that I stopped working altogether. My last day of work was in June, and then I retired. Now I really had time on my hands. I began spending more time on my computer. I began to look up various military websites, and came across one that had the Wall in Washington on it. You could look up names on it, and you could leave a remembrance for anyone that was listed. Since it had been so many years since I was in Vietnam, I couldn't think of very many names, plus the fact that we only knew some guys by a nickname that was used there. So, I looked up the names that I could remember, and wrote a brief message for them. One thing that I noticed was that many names didn't have anything written for them at all. This bothered me a great deal, because I thought this was the every least thing that people could do to acknowledge the sacrifice that they had made, but maybe this was a new website, and people weren't aware of it yet.

Something incredible came out of me doing this. Not too much longer after I wrote them, I was contacted by e-mail from the family of my Corpsman "Doc Ben." They were thrilled that somebody had left a remembrance for their brother, and thanked me for doing so. So, this began a series of e-mails between us. It turned out that his parents had passed away years before, but his one brother had been searching for 34 years to find anyone that knew his brother in Vietnam, and had never found anyone. He even hired a Private Investigator to do a search which also didn't produce any results. I was the first contact that they had ever made. I think we both were a little nervous about this in the beginning, but as time went by we got more comfortable. Two days after the first e-mail contact was made, my doorbell rang, and standing there was a delivery man with two dozen white roses. Initially my wife and daughter thought it was for them because it was Christmas Eve. The Corpsman's Brother, and his family sent them to me, along with a beautiful note. We had exchanged addresses, and phone numbers, but hadn't talked to each other, with the exception of e-mail. So I immediately sent them a thank you note on e-mail, and asked if I could call them on the phone. They agreed to this, and welcomed the opportunity. Once again, we were both pretty nervous about talking to each other. I was worried about what they might ask, and they were probably worried about what my answer might be.

I was definitely scared, but I made the phone call. The Brother's name was Art, and his wife's name was Bonnie. It was difficult at first, just because of all the emotions we both felt. We talked, and talked for about two hours. Their family was from Michigan, and he had been one of five kids. Doc Ben had three older brothers, and a twin sister. Then I told them some things about myself, and my family to get acquainted. After some time had passed, and we both seemed to relax a bit, we talked about their brother. Their questions were made out of concern about how he died, and were there other people with him at the time. The families are never given much information when this occurs. Their respective branch of service sends a representative as an escort with the body, but this is not a person that knew them, and they only have the most basic of information, or details. Usually all this consisted of was what region they died in, and if they knew the manner in which they were killed, an example of this would be by small arms fire. This was a difficult job for anyone and their reactions to you were varied. I had participated in funeral details in California. Here you are facing a family with the worst possible news they will in all likelihood ever receive, and you're only given the minimum of information. The questions Doc Ben's family had for me, were really simple in nature, but had never been addressed in 34 years. They wanted to know some of the circumstances in which he died, was he alone, and did he suffer? I was able to answer these questions for them, because I was twenty feet away from him when it occurred, and witnessed it. My memory of that incident is just as vivid now, as when it happened. We both cried during this phone conversation, but maybe found a sense of peace in recalling these horrific memories.

I think because of our mutual experience we share a lot of the same feelings. We continue to call each other, and we have become very close over the past few years. The following summer my wife and I drove to Michigan to visit them. This was on the 4th of July, and we stayed up there for a few days. The visit brought on a whole new set of emotions. Somehow being face to face for the first time made us nervous, even though we had been talking frequently on the phone for over six months. When we got to their house we just walked up to each other, and hugged. It was like we had known each other our whole lives. There were also a lot of tears shed that day. His twin sister Barb was also there. She had taken the loss of her brother particularly hard, maybe because they were twins, not that it is any better for other siblings, but being a twin you probably felt like half of you also died. When she hugged me I swear I could feel the warmth of her love for her brother, but also the pain she felt for all those years.

We continue to stay in touch with each other, and I'll never forget that first e-mail, that first phone call, or that first embrace. They have given me the honor of acceptance into their family, and they are a part of mine, and always will be.

Sometime later I received another e-mail. This one came from the younger sister of "Little John." She had seen the remembrance that I left for her brother, and decided to contact me. At the time of his death she was a very young girl, and had some of the same questions the other family had. In addition to that, because she was so young at the time it occurred she also wanted to learn more about her brother as a man. Her name is Paula, and she and her family still live in the same town where Little John grew up. This was in North Carolina. I probably had as many questions for her, as she had for me. Her brother was married, and had a son at the time of his death, and I always thought about that young boy growing up without his father. He was just a toddler at the time, and probably no recollection of his father, other than what people may have told him over the years. Looking at a picture without any memory of the person in it doesn't tell you much about that person. I have talked to Paula on the phone a number of times now. She told me that their Mother was still alive, but is suffering from Alzheimer's disease, and that their Father had died shortly after her brother died in Vietnam. She told me that Little John's wife got remarried, and moved to Georgia with their son. So, they haven't seen too much of them over the years. I told Paula that one day we should get together, but as of this time we haven't done that yet. We talk on the phone from time to time, and she always remembers me on every holiday with a card. She, like the family of Doc Ben has become a part of my extended family, and I am so grateful for being able to make the connection with her. One of these days we will get together, and I'm looking forward to it.

Both of these families had their lives turned upside down, and torn apart many years ago by the loss of their loved ones, and they are just two of the over 58000 other families that shared this same experience. The impact of war not only took their loved ones away from them, but has altered the way in which they have lived their lives ever since. Each loss has a ripple effect that reaches out to everyone that was ever a part of their lives, whether they were a brother, a sister, a son, or a friend.

During this time my wife had a stroke. I can't put into words how I felt at the time. She had always been with me, and had been my only support system for all these years. It just never occurred to me that something could happen to her. Fortunately, it wasn't a major stroke, and she recovered. Later we found out that she had two genetic blood disorders, both of which can cause blood clots. As a result of this it was recommended that my daughters be tested, as well as her brother, and sister, and later my grandkids. There is no cure for this as of today, but knowing you have it is half the battle, because there is treatment in the form of blood thinners, but she does have to get her blood tested every couple weeks to monitor the level of her medication.

While playing around on my computer I found a website for the unit I served with in Vietnam A few years earlier several guys had decided to create an organization to represent our Battalion. I contacted them, and decided to join them. By this time they had a few hundred members. This was made up of all the guys that served in Vietnam in this Battalion while it was over there. It would cover the years from 1965 to 1969. Once a year they held a reunion. I attended my first reunion with them in Quantico Virginia which is just outside of Washington. When I first signed up I didn't recognize any names of the people that were members, but thought that by going to the reunion that maybe I might be able to jog loose enough of my memory to remember at least one of them. I tried as hard as I could to remember some names from my past, and looked at some pictures I had from those days. One name rang a bell right away, and that was Paul, aka Fang." I remembered that he lived in Massachusetts. He had kind of an unusual name, so I thought I would see if I could find him. I punched his name and state into my computer white pages, and only one listing popped up. It had to be him, and if it wasn't maybe he was a relative that could put me in touch. That night I called the number, and a woman answered the phone. I stumbled through the explanation of who I was, and who I was looking for. She said that she was his wife, and she would go get him in the other room. I don't know who was surprised more, him or me. We talked for quite awhile, and I told him about the organization I had found from our unit, and that there was an upcoming reunion. He said he would join, and would meet me there. Our wives would also attend.

Not long after my contact with Paul, I got another e-mail from a guy named Art who had gotten my e-mail address from the roster of our organization. He remembered me as well as loads of other information about the time we spent there, and other people that served with us. I told him about Paul, and he remembered him right away. He also called Paul, and they got together since they didn't live very far from each other. Now there were two guys I would know at the reunion.

I was excited when we arrived at the reunion. While I was checking in, Paul walked right up to me, and I was surprised he recognized me, but I sure did recognize him. Art, Paul, and I were inseparable throughout the reunion, but we talked to as many other guys as we could while we were there. We also found another guy that we had served with, and that was Chuck. This was really turning out great. So far all these guys were with me on my second tour, and I hadn't seen anybody from my first tour yet. After awhile, I found a man from my first tour named Clyde. I remembered him because he was from a town that was about fifty miles north of where I lived. Clyde wasn't in Vietnam very long before he got severely wounded, and was sent home. Another guy named Jim had stepped on a mine, and Clyde along with several others, were also wounded. Jim was also here at the reunion, but he was here without the legs he had lost in Vietnam.

We had many long conversations during this reunion about our experiences, and one thing became evident to Paul and Art, and that was I was still having many problems dealing with the war's after-affects. They knew right away that I needed some help, and tried to convince me to get some. I just shrugged it off at the time. One thing that I always feared was that if I tried to get some help that I would end up in another place like I was in Philadelphia, only this time it would be permanent. My wife had always known something was wrong with me as a result of my war experiences, and tried as hard as she could to get me to do something about it. Any time the subject ever came up, I not only wouldn't listen to her, but I would also get very angry. I would fight her over the mere mention of it. No one, no matter how close they were to me, was going to get me to even acknowledge that I had a problem. It would take a couple more reunions, and a whole lot of encouragement by lots of people, and most particularly my wife, to get me to set foot in a VA hospital. I think going to reunions helped loosen the grip of fear that I felt toward seeking treatment. You, as an individual are the one that has to take the first step. No one can do it for you, but the alternative is not having a life at all.

Somewhere in the middle of all this, and before I went to the VA, a day like no other occurred. This was 9-11. That morning my wife, and I boarded a plane to fly down to visit my brother in South Carolina. It was a beautiful day, and we were going to spend a week at my brother's place. Things were going fine, and we were due to arrive in about a half hour. Then the Pilot made an announcement that we were being diverted to Columbia South Carolina. He didn't give any reason for this, and we just figured that Charleston must be experiencing some bad weather, or something. When we landed, the Pilot came back into the cabin, and explained that everyone should get off the plane, and take everything with them, because this flight would be going no further. There was a little grumble at first, but then he said there had been some terrorist activity, and we would receive further information inside the terminal. As we walked in the terminal we saw everybody watching some television screens, and looked up just in time to see the second plane hit the World Trade Center. I'm not sure if it had just happened, or we were watching a replay of the event, but there was a sense of panic in the crowd. My wife went to call our youngest daughter to let her know that we were alright, while I got the rest of our luggage. My daughter was screaming at her for us to get the hell out of the airport. The airline had already made arrangements for us to be driven to Charleston by a shuttle bus. It seemed odd, but they took us to Charleston's Airport. Well that was our destination anyway, and people were waiting for the passengers there. They wouldn't let them drive up to the terminal however. My brother was finally able to pick us up though. So like everyone else, we spent the entire week glued to the television, and we weren't sure if we would be able to, or want to fly home again.

We did get back on a plane a week later, and flew home. The security procedures at the airport were a whole lot different now. Actually we thought this would be a long drawn out process, but so many people were afraid to fly at this time, the airport was fairly empty.

The whole country was gripped with the fear of terrorism, and the feeling of vulnerability, and outrage. We wanted to get even with somebody, and to make them pay for all the lives lost in the carnage. We were at war again, only this time it was right in our own backyard. Just as had been the case in any other war, there were people directly involved, and those that only witnessed it on television. We all felt compassion for the victims, and their families, but in real terms, most of our lives hadn't changed very much.

If you, or a relative, or somebody you knew was on one of those planes, or in one of those buildings, or in close proximity to them, then you felt the full impact of this tragic situation. No matter what everyone else saw, or heard about this event from a distance, they will never know the affect it has had on your life. There are a lot of people there in the beginning, to help you attend to the obvious needs that have to be met, but my concern is for the long range quality of life for those lives that were so abruptly changed

I wasn't there, but I do know something about survival, and sometimes it takes a heavy toll.

Chapter 15

Getting Treatment

The acts of terrorism in this country, and the constant reminders everywhere you turned, made my own nightmares kick up a notch. My sleeping habits were getting worse, and I just didn't feel like doing anything. Somehow my life would have to get better, and I knew this meant that inevitably I would have to do something about it. There was a VA Hospital fairly close to where I lived and I finally decided to go there. This took some time to convince myself, because the more I thought about it, the less I wanted to face it. All the fears and apprehension of what would be waiting for me in doing so would cause me to talk myself out of it on a number of occasions. One morning after a particularly sleepless night I decided that this would be the day. I drove over to the hospital, and just sat in the parking lot for four, or five hours. Finally I walked in, but at this stage I was nearly the same as I was when they sent me out of Vietnam. They immediately brought me into an examination room to see a Doctor. After that everything was kind of a big blur. I remember seeing other Doctors called into see me, along with nurses, and various other members of their staff. I'm not sure how long I was there that day, and I wasn't sure if they were going to let me go home. The big concern was whether or not I felt like killing myself, or someone else. I told them no, that I was here for help. The Doctor gave me a couple of prescriptions. One was to help me sleep, and the other was to help alter my mood swings. They also set me up with a schedule for both individual, and group therapy sessions. Initially I would be going there five days a week. When I got home, I was completely exhausted, and this would be the case every other time I went there.

I had been assigned to one Psychologist for my individual therapy, and he would also moderate the group sessions I attended. I called him "Dr. John." I was barely able to speak during the first few sessions that I had with him on an individual basis, and it would be a whole lot longer before I said anything in the group sessions. At first when I came home from these sessions, my wife thought that they were doing me more harm than good, because of the outward appearance I had when I returned home from them. There was even a group that met once a week for the wives. Doctor John had a calming effect, and was a very good listener. He had been working with Veterans for nearly twenty years. As time passed, I was still nervous about walking in the door, and would get there early, and just sit out in the parking lot, and listen to music for a couple hours. I would relax a bit after that. When I walked into the group for the first time, seeing the other guys that were there was like looking into a mirror. The groups usually contained five, or six of us and Dr. John. It took me a long time to get comfortable enough to speak in the groups, but as I got to know the guys there it became a little easier. The hardest part was reliving all those memories. I remember somebody asking if there was a cure for this, and was told no, but maybe we can help you live a more productive, and rewarding life.

After I had been going to the VA for about four months, I began writing some one page articles, about the various thoughts that I had. I would wake up in the middle of the night, and just write down whatever popped into my head. Some were written in the form of poems, while others were just prose. This served as sort of a self-imposed form of therapy for me. I didn't think they were particularly well written, but after each time I finished one, I felt a sense of relief, and up to this point I had never been able to communicate how I felt in any other fashion. It was as though by putting my thoughts down on paper, I could loose some of the baggage I had been carrying around with me.

I told Dr. John that I had been doing this, and he asked if he could read them. At first I was a little embarrassed by the thought of this, because I had never written anything before this in my entire life. I even told him that I thought they were crap, but I would let him read them anyway. After he read a few, he asked me if he could read them to the group. By this time I had gotten over the embarrassment of letting someone see what I had written, but I was still very nervous about having them read before a group. I finally agreed to let him do this, and just sat there feeling a great deal of apprehension. A strange thing occurred when he did this, most of the guys said these contained a lot of the same thoughts that they had been having, and were also unable to communicate. So each time we had a group session I would bring whatever I had just written, and the Doc would read them to the group. Some of these guys even asked if they could have a copy.

After awhile I began to read them to the group myself. There was another larger group that met more informally once a week on Friday mornings. This was in the unit where guys were admitted for a five week in-patient program. The Doc asked me if I would be interested in going there and reading some of these articles to this larger group. This group contained as many as 50 to 75 men, and on occasion other people would sit in on this meeting. Now I had gone from being unable to say anything to anybody, to reading something I had written in front of groups as large as this. These guys were from all over the country, and would also ask for copies afterward. The emotions of this experience were a little overwhelming. The men in this room were my peers, but maybe they were just trying to encourage another Veteran, and maybe these one page thoughts won't mean anything to anybody else outside of this room, but you never know.

The remaining pages in this chapter are some of those one page thoughts that I had written. I don't know if they will make any sense to anyone that wasn't part of this experience, but they may offer some insight into what happens to the human spirit as a result of war. They range from one called "Walking through the Door" which is what I thought about going to the VA the first time, to "Life Outside the Bunker" which is a look at the frustrating lives of some Veterans. Some of these were written from fear some from frustration, and some were written with a desire to change the outcome of what had been my life.

Walking Through the Door

TOOK THIRTY YEARS TO GET HERE
DON'T KNOW WHAT'S ON THE OTHER SIDE
FACE TO FACE WITH DEMONS OF THE PAST
INTRUSIVE THOUGHTS OF THOSE THAT DIED

DO I WALK THROUGH THE DOOR FACING ME
OR IS IT EASIER JUST TO WALK AWAY
DOESN'T SEEM LIKE MUCH OF A CHOICE
IF IT'S TOO UNCOMFORTABLE DO I HAVE TO STAY

PEOPLE HAVE SAID YOU NEED SOME HELP
WHO THE HELL DO THEY THINK THEY ARE
THEY DON'T KNOW ANYTHING ABOUT ME
BE A HELL OF LOT EASIER TO DROWN IN A BAR

THERE'S A LOT MORE HERE THAN WHAT THEY SEE
UNDERNEATH A PERSON WISHING THEY COULD FEEL
STUCK IN A PLACE FOR WHICH THERE IS NO ESCAPE
STILL JUST A BOY NOT A MAN MADE OF STEEL

THE HARDEST PART IS WALKING THROUGH THE DOOR
FACES ALL TOO FAMILIAR IT'S LIKE LOOKING IN A MIRROR
FINALLY FOUND OTHERS THAT KNOW WHAT I'M ABOUT
NOW MAYBE MY THOUGHTS WILL BECOME CLEARER

Written by George Brondsema

Thin Skin

People often describe others as having "Thin Skin." This would imply that they are over sensitive or unwilling to conform to standards accepted by the majority of people. They seem to be perceived as being difficult in their relationship to others. This oversimplification of terms, in reality contributes to these feelings, rather than to explain them.

In our lifetime, we are faced with many challenges. How we deal with them makes us who we will become. It's easy to say "I would have done this in that situation," but the reality is, we don't know what we would have done. It's like another expression often used, and that is "walking in someone else's shoes."

Each obstacle we face, whether serious in nature or not, makes, us what we are. When they are serious, it's like having a layer of skin peeled away. When this occurs, we are left with a feeling of vulnerability. Anyone that has gone through difficult times has gotten a little thinner skinned. These feelings often stay with us, and will shadow our lives.

Veterans, as a group are exposed to this type of scrutiny. They have been placed in situations that would alter the thinking of even the strongest personalities, yet when they act differently than the rest of us, we act surprised. They are often treated as more of an oddity, or annoyance, rather than with the compassion, dignity, respect, and understanding they so richly deserve. Their many layers of skin were peeled away early in life, leaving them especially vulnerable. As a result, many of them withdrew into a lonely existence, one of isolation, anger, and confusion. To this, our reaction has often been to tell them to "get over it."

Yes Veterans are "Thin Skinned"

Written by George Brondsema

You're Not Alone

SITTING ALONE IN A DARKENED ROOM
YOUR THOUGHTS FIXED ON THE PAST
SHOULD BE A TRANQUIL SETTING
BUT YOUR MIND IS RACING FAST

SHADOWS AND IMAGES FLYING BY
WHO IS THIS WHAT WAS THAT
YOU FEEL YOUR HEART POUNDING
NOTHING NEW I KNOW WHERE I'M AT

FEELINGS OF RAGE FOLLOWED BY GUILT
NOBODY SEEMS TO CARE ARE THEY ALL BLIND
CLOSING MY EYES DOESN'T SOLVE A THING
A LACK OF PEACE IS ALL THAT I FIND

AN EXISTANCE WHERE A LIFE SHOULD HAVE BEEN
PAIN FROM A WOUND THAT DOESN'T BLEED
SHUT OFF FROM THE WORLD AROUND ME
WON'T TALK TO OTHERS, DON'T FEEL THE NEED

WHEN AT LAST THIS LIFE IS OVER FOR ME
AND I JOIN THE FACES MY MIND CAST IN STONE
I WILL FIND THE PEACE I WAS ALWAYS LOOKING FOR
BECAUSE HERE THEY NEVER LEFT ME ALONE

Written by George Brondsema

Soul of War

No matter how a war begins, there is never an end. Once initiated it develops a personality of its own, as if were a living being. As time goes by, it develops an appetite for those that participate in its life. War is like a disease, it grows on the bodies, and minds of its participants, consuming them with a furor that is insatiable.

War does not discriminate it is an equal opportunity possessor of souls. It makes no distinction whether you are black or white, male or female, young or old. If you are a participant, war will also attach itself to the lives of your family. This infection reaches out like a ripple on a pond, eventually infecting everyone you come in contact with.

The life of a Veteran is spent in long nights, and endless days, staring into the face of this all consuming soul of war. It seems strange that what started out as a single event in your life will become a lifetime battle of wills for your soul. Sometimes with the help of others, you may make a truce with your memories, but in the long run, war will not allow you to deny your past. War has been called "hell," and perhaps it is, but we won't have the answer to that, until the soul of war no longer possesses our soul.

Written by George Brondsema

Don't Mean Nothin'

AN ATTITUDE OF THE MIND
A FEELING OF FATE
NO WAY TO CHANGE IT
ALREADY TOO LATE

LOST CONTROL OF LIFE
A FEELING OF DESPAIR
THE WAY LIFE IS
ASK ME IF I CARE

DON'T REMEMBER MUCH
ALWAYS THE SAME
NOTHING IS DIFFERENT
NOBODYS TO BLAME

LIFE IS OVERWHELMING
SOMETHING NEVER TAUGHT
TOO MANY EXPERIENCES
NO TIME FOR THOUGHT

JUST THE WAY IT IS
NOTHING BUT A GAME
DON'T GIVE A DAM
MIGHT AS WELL BE LAME

CAN'T SEE A FUTURE
WHAT WOULD THAT BE
DON'T MEAN NOTHIN'
IS ALL I CAN SEE

Written by George Brondsema

Shattered Lives

When a child is born, we think of this event as a milestone in our lives, an experience where mere words cannot fully describe our feelings. This new life is unlimited in its potential, and is held safe and secure by its family. As in a book, this life will be made up of many chapters.

In the early stages, the family attends to the basic needs that will support life. In this chapter things can be somewhat hectic, as you learn what it takes to be a parent. As with most of life's experiences, you just have to go through it to understand it.

As the child grows into their own being, we have to make adjustments in our lives to accommodate this growth. It can be somewhat difficult to allow this to happen, since up to this point, we have made all their decisions for them.

When your child makes the choice to serve their country, you are filled with both pride, and fear at the same time. This is one of those areas in life that cannot be prepared for. You cannot conceive that they may never return.

If you experience the loss of a child in war, your life ends with theirs. Initially, there may be an outpouring of support for you, but as with most things in life, this will end fairly soon, and then all you're left with is your memories. You will spend the balance of your life asking questions, for which there are no answers. You will wonder what might have been, if this hadn't occurred in your life. You will become angry, and bitter at other people that aren't feeling the same way as you do. You will feel out of touch, and if you are religious you will be angry with God! You will ask why me, and there will be absolutely no one that will understand what you're going through, except for the Veteran that served alongside your child.

Written by George Brondsema

Prison

WHAT TIME IS IT
DON'T REALLY CARE
IT'S ALWAYS THE SAME
UNABLE TO SHARE

DAYS INTO NIGHTS
AND NIGHTS INTO DAYS
MOST OF MY LIFE
SPENT IN A HAZE

MUST BE LIFE OUT THERE
AS I SIT AND STARE
AINT GONNA HAPPEN
CAUSE I DON'T CARE

TIME KEEPS GOING BY
YOU START TO FEEL IT
THEN YOU PULL BACK
AND ASK YOURSELF WHY

TIME IS A MEASUREMENT
PRECISE AND EXACT
YOU'RE ONLY GIVEN SO MUCH
AND THAT IS A FACT

IF WASTING TIME IS A CRIME
THEN I'M GUILTY AS SIN
SO SHOOT ME OR WORSE YET
START THE CLOCK OVER AGAIN

THIS IS MY LIFE
I OFFER NO REPENTANCE
YOU SEE I'M A VETERAN
AND THIS IS MY SENTENCE

Written by George Brondsema

A Shell

A shell can serve many purposes. We can see it as a protective covering for an egg, or maybe as the outside armor of a turtle. They are also used as a means of protection for many other animals. Without this, the life of the animal inside would cease to exist.

A shell can also mean something used to destroy life. This would include such things as an explosive artillery projectile, or a small arms cartridge. It can also be used as a term for the act of firing upon a target, as in "we were shelling the enemy."

A shell can also mean something empty, or spent, or devoid of its contents. In human terms we can take substance from all these meanings, and adapt them to the life's journey of a Veteran. At the beginning our shell protects us and our inner being. This consists of our hopes, dreams, ambitions, and aspirations, for without this we would cease to exist. We are then put in a place where we use shells to destroy other life. After having to suffer this indignation of what we call war, we are empty, hollow, spent, and devoid of our former inner being.

In the end, some may find the ability to restore some of what was lost, but for many of us, life will be like the shell that washes up on the beach, empty, spent, and devoid of content, yet we are still here.

Written by George Brondsema

Keep Going Back

FOR MOST LIFE MOVES FORWARD
BUT I'M STUCK IN THE SAME TRACK
I'M NOT LIKE THE REST
I KEEP GOING BACK

IT ISN'T LIKE I HAVE A CHOICE
OR PLAN OF ATTACK
I JUST CAN'T HELP MYSELF
I KEEP GOING BACK

WHY DO I GO THERE
NOBODY EVER CUT ME SOME SLACK
AIN'T SUPPOSED TO BE THIS WAY, BUT
I KEEP GOING BACK

WHAT AM I LOOKING FOR
IS THERE SOMETHING I LACK
STILL CAUGHT IN THIS WEB
I KEEP GOING BACK

CAN'T TAKE YOU WITH ME
THERES NO NEED TO PACK
IT'S MY PRIVATE JOURNEY, AND
I KEEP GOING BACK

I'M A VETERAN LOST IN HIS PAST
PAINFUL MEMORIES PILED IN A STACK
PRAY I MIGHT FIND PEACE BUT TILL THEN
I KEEP GOING BACK

Written by George Brondsema

Tour of Duty

A tour of duty is a measurement in time. This implies a beginning and an end. Used in a military context, this can be your total length of time served, or as a temporary assignment. Either way, there is a specific time reference made.

In time of war, these references become clouded due to the experiences of war itself. As an example, when someone is killed in the line of action, a tour of duty lasts forever. For someone that is severely wounded, or suffers the loss of a limb, a tour of duty will become a lifetime sentence. Most surviving Veterans will be forced to deal with horrific memories that will last the balance of their lives. These memories will also change the way in which they relate to other people, as well as their surroundings. The burden of survival will outweigh the benefit of life itself.

Throughout life we have used measurements as a guideline, and a means of making things fit. We even measure a man not only on his size, but also on his qualities, and attributes. The latter is based upon a personal judgment, or opinion. A tour of duty in time of war cannot be measured, since it only has a beginning, and where there is no end. This meaning would also apply in attempting to measure the life of a Veteran, but please reserve your judgment and opinions, until you yourself have served a "tour of duty."

Written by George Brondsema

Shadows

DON'T GET TO SLEEP MUCH
TOO MANY SHADOWS IN MY HEAD
FACES FROM LONG AGO
LIVING WITH THE DEAD

MUST PAY HOMAGE TO THESE SOULS
WHEN NO ONE ELSE WILL
THEY DESERVE AT LEAST THIS
I'VE BEEN GIVEN THE BILL

THEY ARE ALWAYS WITH ME
EVERY DAY AND EVERY NIGHT
LIFETIME COMPANIONS
STEALING MY SIGHT

THEY WANT TO SHARE IN MY LIFE
IS THIS TOO MUCH TO ASK
AS LONG AS I'M HERE
I HAVE TO ACCEPT THIS TASK

THEY ARE MY WORLD
THEY WEREN'T GIVEN A CHOICE
SOMEONE HAS TO REMEMBER
I AM THEIR VOICE

THEIR MEMORY WILL NEVER FAD
AS TOGETHER WE GROW OLD
SHADOWS OF WAR
THEIR STORY MUST BE TOLD

Written by George Brondsema

Waging War

Waging war is a curious term for such a life altering experience. The term "wages" implies a payment given for services rendered. What would be a fair wage for those called upon to fight in a war? Most of the people that are directly involved are paid at a poverty level. If the decision makers of the country were directly involved in the fighting what would they feel was an acceptable wage? I suppose they would quote sayings such as "freedom isn't free," and other superlatives. Although, there is truth in these sayings, the freedom is only paid by the Veteran, his family, and friends.

There is another form of payment, and that is of life, and limb. Curiously they even assign a dollar figure to these losses. I wonder what these people would take in trade for an arm or a leg, let alone their life. The myriad of injuries aren't limited to these few examples. Anyone that has ever fought in the name of their country knows only too well what has been paid. For many the mental anguish of their experience lives in the forefront of their minds for the rest of their life. So what is a "fair wage?"

Long as there have been people on this earth, there have been wars. In this regard history continues to repeat itself. One thing for sure, whenever we decide to wage war, we need to give some thought to the people that do the fighting. Ammunition and equipment cost nothing in comparison to the human cost. Veterans aren't liabilities on a balance sheet.

If we are still intent on dealing only with dollars and cents, then we should budget ourselves with integrity. For the Veterans, put a dollar away, for every dollar spent on waging war!

"A Fair Wage."

Written by George Brondsema

Age

EVER LOOK IN A MIRROR
AN OLD MAN LOOKING BACK
NO RECOGNITION OF HIS FACE
APPEARS LOST WITHOUT A TRACE

NOTHING LOOKS FAMILIAR
LIFE HAS PASSED HIM BY
MAD AS HELL WHERE DID IT GO
THERE IS NOTHING LEFT TO SHOW

HOW MUCH TIME IS LEFT
A QUESTION WITHOUT AN ANSWER
LOST YOUTH IS A SHAME
BUT WHO IS TO BLAME

I SEE A UNIFORM OLD AND WORN
COVERED WITH BLOOD OF BATTLES PAST
WHY DID LIFE BRING ME HERE
ALWAYS THE THOUGHT OF FEAR

SOME THINGS NEVER CHANGE
MAYBE THIS IS LIFE FOR ME
THIS STORY WAS NEVER FORETOLD
BUT HELL I'M ONLY EIGHTEEN YEARS OLD

Written by George Brondsema

What Might Have Been

It would have been nice to have fought in a popular war. For the most part, previous veterans were treated with respect. This unfortunately was not the case in Vietnam. The odd thing is that the Vietnam Veteran was, and is not responsible for creating that war, although that seems to be the implication in terms of guilt. That decision was made by the previous generation of Veterans.

As is the case in any war, Vietnam was made up of thousands of small stories experienced by a few. The disturbing thing that keeps coming up however is the atrocities that were supposedly perpetrated by everyone involved. Maybe it's too late to change this misconception, but for the sake of the over fifty-eight thousand that cannot speak for themselves I hope this is not true. In the time I spent in Vietnam the behavior of the people I served with, was one of dignity, pride, compassion, and selflessness under extremely difficult circumstances.

Since the news media's main focus is profit, they seek out only the most bizarre stories that will feed the feeble minds of the curious, and line their wallets. It seems that the normal horrors of war aren't enough. Over the past thirty-five years, we Veterans have been put in a position of defending ourselves against the onslaught of inaccurate and misrepresented facts that have been circulated about the conduct of Veterans. In their view, if it happened once, then it was widespread.

If in fact you are one of their sources of this type of information, and claim that you either did some of these acts, or witnessed them and did nothing, then in my view you are not a Veteran, but merely a common criminal, and should be treated as such. We as Veterans have had to tolerate the intolerable, not only in time of war, but every day since that time.

Written by George Brondsema

A Choice

HELL IS FOR HEROES
IT'S ONLY A SURVIVORS PAIN
SOMETHING ALWAYS WITH YOU
YES BLOOD DOES LEAVE A STAIN

DROWNING IN ALCOHOL
NUMBING WITH DRUGS
LIFETIME OF DEPRESSION
DON'T GET ANY HUGS

ONLY FRIEND IS ANGER
WOULD BE EASIER IF YOU DIED
NOTHING BUT FRUSTRATION
NO ONE KNOWS YOU CRIED

SWIMMING IN OLD MEMORIES
DROWNING IN THE PAST
TOTAL LACK OF HAPPINESS
YOU PUT YOURSELF DEAD LAST

HAS TO GET BETTER THAN THIS
NEED TO GET A VOICE
NO WAY TO LIVE IN THIS LIFE
I NEED TO MAKE A CHOICE

Written by George Brondsema

Hell in Survival

There is an assumption made that if you are a survivor, then the worst is over. In reality it is just the beginning. In war, the incident, or action may have only lasted mere seconds, but the aftermath can be eternal. There are several definitions of the word "Veteran," and after looking them up I found the first definition given is "old and experienced." The second example is "a person of long service in some position." The final example given is "one who has served in the armed forces." I find it ironic, that the last example given was what I thought would be the first. Then I thought for a moment, and came to realize that the other two examples are an uncanny description of the subsequent life of the Veteran survivor. Being old and experienced, and a person of long service in some position accurately reflect the outlook, the feeling, and quality of life for the survivor.

It had always been my idea that a Veteran was and is a survivor. Understand that war is played out much like a game. We keep score in terms of lives lost, and injured on both sides. In order to become proficient at this game we train like athletes. We prepare both physically, and mentally to reach the best of our ability. When the time arrives we pray that this will see us through.

There is however, one thing that is completely overlooked. In all this training, and preparation for going into battle, not one minute is ever spent on what it's like to survive. No matter how many times this country has participated in various wars throughout history, we have yet to learn about the longest segment of fighting a war, and that is the hell that awaits in survival.

Written by George Brondsema

Helpless Feeling

WHO DO YOU TURN TO
WHAT DO YOU SAY
WHO CAN YOU TALK TO
JUST HAVE TO LIVE FOR TODAY

TIME TOGETHER SPENT ALONE
WHO COULD YOU CALL ANYWAY
COULD USE SOME SUPPORT
JUST HAVE TO LIVE FOR TODAY

HOLDING LIFE TOGETHER
EACH AND EVERY DAY
CAN'T THINK ABOUT TOMORROW
JUST HAVE TO LIVE FOR TODAY

BEEN LIKE THIS FOR YEARS
LIKE A ROLE IN A PLAY
UP AND DOWN WITHOUT WARNING
JUST HAVE TO LIVE FOR TODAY

YOU NEVER GIVE UP THOUGH
ALTHOUGH SOMETIMES YOU PRAY
YOU'RE THE WIFE OF A VETERAN
THANK GOD YOU LIVE FOR TODAY

Written by George Brondsema

Above and Beyond

I find difficulty in trying to determine what exactly is "above and beyond" when referring to the call of duty. These words are generally used as a description of an individual's action witnessed by others. This however, falls into the category of a perceived judgment made by the witness. So in order to do something that would be considered above and beyond, there needs to be a witness.

From what source does the witness get the information necessary to determine what is considered above and beyond? You have to ask yourself then, what is the basic call to duty? While training for military service you are asked to perform various tasks. Some of these would be considered tedious, and mundane, while others would be tense, and exciting. Then there is a built-in element of danger to the individual called upon to perform the job for which they were trained. With this in mind, what then becomes above and beyond?

I am left with a very simple truth, and that is when a person enters the service of their country, they have answered the call of duty, and when they are called upon to do the job for which they were trained, all else should be considered as above, and beyond.

Written by George Brondsema

Veteran Reflections

STUCK IN THE PAST
HOW LONG WILL IT LAST
DO I LIKE WHAT I SEE
WHEN I LOOK BACK AT ME

COMPANIONS OF FEAR AND PAIN
A LIFE I CAN'T REGAIN
SPEND MY TIME IN GRIEF
WITH LITTLE OR NO RELIEF

NO WAY TO LIVE
NOTHING LEFT TO GIVE
THOUGHT I DID MY BEST
IF ONLY I COULD REST

ARE THERE MORE LIKE ME
PEOPLE THAT CANNOT SEE
FACES WITHOUT A VOICE
AS IF THEY HAD A CHOICE

IT WAS MY DECISION
MAYBE A LACK OF VISION
STILL NO REGRET
JUST AN UNENDING DEBT

BECAUSE OF PEOPLE LIKE ME
THEY SAY WE ARE FREE
BUT DO I LIKE WHAT I SEE
WHEN I LOOK BACK AT ME

Written by George Brondsema

There Are No Heroes

There are no heroes, there are only heroic acts. I looked up the definitions, and I am at odds with the example given. It implies that a hero is someone with a willingness to perform a heroic act. I don't believe anyone is capable of knowing whether or not they would be able to perform such an act. Heroic acts are an involuntary reaction to a situation that suddenly presents itself. This is much like the blink of an eye.

Many of us have pondered the question of how we would react to a given situation. If we are being paid to perform a dangerous job willingly, are we then heroes or does some defining situation have to present itself first? Having made this case then is it a judgment call, or is there some criteria to be met?

What seems strange about all this is that the majority of people who perform these heroic acts will never know that they were considered heroes. I saw a man jump on a grenade for which he was awarded the Medal of Honor. In the citation it was stated that by his action, many other lives were saved. This is undeniably true, but I can't help but wonder though, if this man had the time to process the thought of what his final outcome would be, would he have done the same thing?

Heroism is an unknown quantity or quality whichever you prefer. I choose to think that this is a quality, but we cannot predict who will react in this manner. Therefore, I believe anyone that serves for the common good of his fellow man is indeed a hero. For those of you in the service, I salute you, and ask you to please take the time to look at the people that you are serving with. One may save your life, and you will never guess what each one is capable of.

Written by George Brondsema

Incoming

A SOUND OFTEN HEARD
A JOLT TO THE HEART
A PARALIZED MIND
BUT WHO WILL IT FIND

IT HAPPENS SO FAST
YET ANTICIPATION IS SLOW
I'M NOT READY FOR THIS
NO WHERE TO GO

DON'T LET IT BE ME
FROZEN WITH SWEAT
I'M WAY TO YOUNG
NO TIME FOR REGRET

WHOSE NUMBER DOES IT SEEK
TOO LATE TO WORRY NOW
SOME SAY OH WELL
SOMEBODY HAS TO PAY IN HELL

THERE GOES THE SOUND
LOOKS LIKE IT MISSED
LUCKY DAY FOR US
WE'RE STILL AROUND

CANCEL THAT THOUGHT
HERE COMES ANOTHER
GETTING OLD, BEGINNING TO TIRE
OH MY GOD, HERE COMES THE FIRE

Written by George Brondsema

Can't Explain It

THEY ASK WHAT WAS IT LIKE
WHEN YOU WENT TO WAR
HOW DO YOU EXPLAIN IT
THEY WANT TO KNOW MORE

WORDS WON'T DO IT JUSTICE
IN THE HELL YOU WENT THROUGH
IT'S LIKE DESCRIBING TO A BLIND MAN
THE COLOR OF BLUE

TOO MANT SENSES INVOLVED IN A WAR
SENSE OF SMELL THEY WON'T COMPREHEND
SOUNDS THEY HAVE NEVER HEARD
SIGHTS OF THINGS THAT NEVER END

A PICTURE PAINTED WITH MEMORIES
THE CANVAS LIES WITHIN YOUR MIND
UNABLE TO DESCRIBE THIS TO ANYONE
A FEELING OF BEING LEFT BEHIND

SO IN ANSWER TO YOUR QUESTIONS
THERE IS NO WAY TO EXPLAIN
JUST KNOW THAT EVERY VETERAN
IS SUFFERING IN SILENT PAIN

Written by George Brondsema

Battle Blindness

EYES WITHOUT A VISION
LIFE WITHOUT A PURPOSE
ONCE FELT YOUNG AND BOLD
BUT NOW I'M JUST FEELING OLD

LIFES A STRUGGLE EVERYDAY
JUST TRYING TO FIND MY WAY
IT SEEMS I'VE GIVEN UP ON ME
LIKE THERE'S NOTHING LEFT TO SEE

EXCITEMENT HAS GONE OUT OF MY LIFE
HOW DO YOU EXPLAIN THIS TO A WIFE
AS A PARENT I'M NOT THE SAME
I WON'T BE MAKING THE HALL OF FAME

EVERYDAY LIFE SEEMS TO ESCAPE ME
FEELINGS OF THE PAST WON'T LET ME FREE
PEACE SHOULD FEEL TRANQUIL AS A FOUNTAIN
BUT I LOST MINE YEARS AGO ON A MOUNTAIN

EYES MELTED SHUT TO THE WORLD AROUND ME
BATTLES LONG AGO HAVE TAKEN MY ABILITY TO SEE
JUST THOUGHTS BURNED INTO MEMORY NEVER
ENDING
WALKING A NARROW PATH WITHOUT BENDING

Written by George Brondsema

Mist on the Mountain

YOU'RE ON TOP OF THE MOUNTAIN
A VISION YOUR EYES CANNOT SEE
YOUR BREATH IS WITHHELD BY FEAR
THE FACE OF DEATH IS NEAR

WHO WOULD IT CALL UPON TODAY
HAVE I DONE EVERYTHING I COULD
DO I HAVE A REASON FOR LIVING
HOW CAN LIFE BE SO UNFORGIVING

THE SILENCE HERE IS DEAFENING
JUST THE BEATING OF MY HEART
SWEAT ROLLING DOWN MY FACE
SOMEBODY WON'T LEAVE THIS PLACE

AS A MAN WHAT ARE YOU WORTH
NO TIME TO PONDER THAT QUESTION
MAYBE GOD WILL LET YOU STAY
BUT THEN AGAIN BOTH SIDES PRAY

THE MIST IS ON THE MOUNTAIN
IT IS NEITHER FOG OR CLOUD
JUST RISING SOULS THAT WERE TAKEN
THE REMAINING WILL BE FORSAKEN

Written by George Brondsema

In Your Name

IN YOUR NAME, Young men and women have answered the call to defend freedom throughout the world. They have given their lives, their youth, their minds, and bodies to this country, and it's commitment to freedom. For many the burden of battle doesn't end with their homecoming. Their lives have been forever changed both physically, and mentally forever. For some the daily challenges of life itself will become a greater battle than the one fought on a foreign shore.

Like everyone else these young people have, or had families. For one moment imagine what it is like to be the Father, Mother, Brother, or Sister of one of these Veterans? What if they were your Husband, or Wife? What goes through the mind of a child when they see what happens to their Father or Mother? They also fight the battle alongside their loved ones. How does one prepare for this experience? There is no way to prepare.

IN THEIR NAME, Your obligation should be to remember them everyday, not just on Veteran's Day. They have given of themselves in a way that you will never know or fully appreciate. These lives have been offered to you to maintain a lifestyle that is often taken for granted. They have made possible the very existence of a country where you can live,

and share in these fundamental freedoms. They deserve your honor, respect, compassion, caring, and love, just as unconditional as the sacrifice they made.
IN YOUR NAME

Written by George Brondsema

Baggage

BAGGAGE IS A BURDEN
THAT YOU CARRY EVERYDAY
A WEIGHT UPON YOUR SHOULDERS
A DEBT THAT YOU MUST PAY

IT'S FILLED WITH MEMORIES
SOME GOOD AND SOME BAD
A LIFETIME COLLECTION
OF EXPERIENCES YOU'VE HAD

THE BAD ONES ARE HEAVY
THE GOOD ONES SEEM LIGHT
IT'S A MATTER OF PERCEPTION
A STRUGGLE WITH YOUR SIGHT

WEAKENED BY THE WEIGHT
MORE THAN YOU CAN BEAR
IF ONLY THERE WAS SOMEONE
WITH THIS BURDEN YOU COULD SHARE

THE THOUGHTS OF A VETERAN
WORDS THAT WERE NEVER SPOKEN
TOO MUCH BAGGAGE TO CARRY
A MAN THAT WAS LEFT BROKEN

Written by George Brondsema

Too Young

STAINED BY LOST HOPE AND PROMISES
MOST OF THEM STILL IN THEIR TEENS
FACES TOO YOUNG TOO SHORT OF LIFE
REALITY FOR THEM CUTS LIKE A KNIFE

NOT OLD ENOUGH TO CAST A VOTE
CAN'T LEGALLY BUY A BEER
MAYBE THERE'S A GIRL IN HIS LIFE
ALTHOUGH MOST NEVER HAD A WIFE

NEVER BOUGHT A BRAND NEW CAR
BUT KNEW EXACTLY THE ONE YOU WANTED
NOTHING UNUSUAL JUST A TYPICAL TEEN
BUT NOW HAUNTED BY WHAT HE HAS SEEN

MEMORIES OF HORRORS FROZEN IN TIME
GOING HOME WITHOUT RECOGNITION
TOO MANY INJURIES TOO MANY KILLED
AN OATH TO GOD AND COUNTRY FULFILLED

VETERANS ARE OFTEN TAKEN FOR GRANTED
SEEMS STRANGE FROM A COUNTRY SO BLESSED
YOU ARE THE RECIPIENT OF MANY THINGS
JUST NEVER FORGET THEY ALL COME WITH STRINGS

Written by George Brondsema

Feeling of Pride

A CALL TO ARMS
THAT FEELING OF PRIDE
I'M BECOMING A MAN
HONOR YOU CANNOT HIDE

THE EXPERIENCE OF WAR
TOO MANY HAVE DIED
NOT WHAT YOU THOUGHT
HAS SOMEBODY LIED

LONG AFTER THE WAR
I'M TRYING TO HIDE
CAN'T GET IT BACK
THAT FEELING OF PRIDE

PEOPLE SEEM DISTANT
NOBODY'S ON MY SIDE
LIFE ISN'T WORTH LIVING
IF I DON'T HAVE MY PRIDE

LIFE IS A STRUGGLE
FOR A MIND THAT IS FRIED
A LIFETIME SPENT SEARCHING
FOR THAT FEELING OF PRIDE

Written by George Brondsema

Life Lost

THERE ONCE WAS A KID
WITH DREAMS TO SHARE
NO END IN SIGHT
LIFE WITHOUT A CARE

FAMILY AROUND HIM
FIGURED THIS WILL ALWAYS BE
LIFE IS GOOD NO NEED TO WORRY
HIS FUTURE IS YET TO SEE

ONE DAY HE WENT TO WAR
NOT KNOWING WHAT WILL BE
THINGS HE KNEW FOR CERTAIN
WERE CHANGED FOREVER MORE

NOW ALL AROUND HIM IS ONLY PAIN
GETTING THROUGH ANOTHER DAY
LIVING THROUGH ANOTHER NIGHT
WILL BECOME HIS LIFE'S REFRAIN

NOW HE FEELS THE NUMBNESS
WILL IT EVER LEAVE HIM
WILL HE EVER CARE
ALL HE HAS LEFT IS JUST A STARE

PEOPLE SAY GET OVER IT
WHAT HAPPENED TO YOU
YOU WEREN'T LIKE THIS BEFORE
I DON'T KNOW YOU ANYMORE

I'D LIKE TO TELL YOU HE SAID
DO YOU REALLY WANT TO KNOW
JUST BETWEEN YOU AND ME
I'M ALREADY DEAD

Written by George Brondsema

When Does it End

WAR IS OVER THEY SAY
THEY MUST NOT MEAN TODAY
SHOULD BE HAPPY YOU'RE ALIVE
A THOUGHT MY MIND CAN'T CONTRIVE

YOU MADE IT BACK
HOW CAN YOU COMPLAIN
ALONE WITH MY THOUGHTS
AND FEELING SUCH PAIN

YOUR FAITH SHOULD BE STRONG
I WOULD LIKE TO BELIEVE
A LUXURY I THINK
BUT CANNOT CONCEIVE

FACES FOREVER LOCKED IN MY HEAD
ALL OF THEM YOUNG
FULL OF LIFE'S PROMISES
YET ALL OF THEM DEAD

I ASK WHY THEM AND NOT ME
DID THEY DO SOMETHING WRONG
DID I DO SOMETHING RIGHT
NO ANSWER TO THIS PLEA

FOR FAMILIES LEFT BEHIND
A VOID THAT CAN'T BE FILLED
THE WORLD NEEDS TO KNOW
INDIFFERENCE IS UNKIND

MAYBE IT'LL GO AWAY SOMEDAY
BUT NOT TODAY
WHEN DOES IT END
WHEN DOES IT END

Written by George Brondsema

We Regret to Inform

A LOSS TO REPORT
WORDS THAT LIVE FOREVER
WORN ON FACES THAT REMEMBER
WORDS THAT MEAN NEVER

AS A PARENT YOU WERE THERE
SINCE THE DAY OF HIS BIRTH
UNCONDITIONAL LOVE
TOO MUCH GRIEF TO BEAR

HE WAS A HUSBAND A FRIEND
A LOVER A SPOUSE
NOW WHO AM I
ALONE IN THIS HOUSE

HE WAS YOUR BROTHER
DIDN'T ALWAYS GET ALONG
NOW I MISS HIM
FOR HE WAS LIKE NO OTHER

HE WAS MY FATHER
WILL I EVER NO WHAT I LOST
WHO WILL PROTECT ME
FOR ME TOO GREAT A COST

A GOOD FRIEND IS SOMETHING RARE
WE SHARED GOOD TIMES AND BAD
CAN'T THINK ABOUT NEVER
ONLY KNOW THAT I'M SAD

A COMRADE IN ARMS
A FOREIGN LAND WE WERE SENT
WILL NEVER FORGET YOU BUDDY
WE BORE WITNESS TO THE EVENT

Written by George Brondsema

Life Outside the Bunker

The purpose of building a bunker is to make a place where you can be safe and secure from harm. The protection it offers is intended as only a temporary solution to the circumstances you are currently facing. The first time you build one, you put all the effort into it that an Architect would us in constructing a skyscraper. Strange as it seems, as time goes by, you put less effort into it. It's as though you start to believe the statement that if they're going to get me, then they're going to get me, and no matter what I do won't change that. No matter what effort you put into them, they do offer a small amount of comfort.

If you survive and return home, you find yourself looking for another form of bunker. This is one you don't build, but reside in nevertheless. It varies from individual to individual, and they can be found in a basement, a garage, a bedroom, or a kitchen. The location is really unimportant. The only thing that really matters is that this place has no other human contact. The reality is that this is more of a state of mind that lies somewhere between your past, and your present.

The ironic thing is that what once was used as a means of protection, now imprisons you. In an odd sort of way it still might give you a sense of comfort, and security. Maybe life is passing you by, but you'll never know for certain till your mind is willing to crawl out of the darkness and into the life outside the bunker.

Written by George Brondsema

Chapter 16

Life Today

For most of my adult life I had wanted to move somewhere else. I thought by moving that I could change what my life had been. The thought of starting over always appealed to me. When I moved thirty miles north of where I grew up, it only served as a temporary fix. It was a good area, and we had a nice house there, but it wasn't enough of a change for me. I think part of the reason that I wanted to go somewhere else is because there was a feeling that you could be whoever you wanted to be, because you could leave your old baggage behind, and nobody would know anything about you. Every time we went anywhere I would pick up all the local real estate ads and study them. I would run the idea of living in this particular place through my mind, and try to envision what it would be like to live there. There was always one constant though, and that was it had to be a hot climate. I had been to Arizona, California, South Carolina, and part of Florida looking for that right place.

In April of 2003 we made a trip to southwest Florida. It was supposed to be just a one week vacation to lie around on the beach. We had a rainy day, and my wife suggested that we go check out some local real estate. I guess my thoughts had rubbed off on her over the years, because it was me that usually made these suggestions. It's a strange thing, we always hear about teenage runaways. They are often running away to find a different life, that is sometimes the result of a bad environment at home, and probably for a lot of other reasons known only to themselves. I was now in my middle fifties, and doing essentially the same thing.

We had never been to this part of Florida before, and really didn't know anything about the area, but after a couple days we put a deposit down on a new home here. After all the years of thinking about doing something like this we even surprised ourselves by making this commitment. I think when we went home, and told our kids that we were going to do this, that they were somewhat surprised. They had heard me talk about this many times over the years, but probably figured it was just some more talk again. We wouldn't be moving until the following year, and that would be in June. So now we had a lot of time to think about it, and sort of digest the whole thing. The time seemed to go by very slowly, and I couldn't believe that we had actually done this

Moving in and of itself, is quite an undertaking. We had made local moves before, but nothing like this. As most people come to find out, when you have been married a long time, and lived in the same place, you tend to accumulate a lot of stuff, and we had our share. The next year we would spend sorting through it, and deciding what would make the trip, and what would stay. I would see some things that I hadn't seen in probably twenty or thirty years that had been packed away, and that we held onto for reasons that escape me now.

Well, we moved, and now we are Floridians. One subject that quietly came up was the possibility of hurricanes. This is something I was unfamiliar with, because you don't see them in Illinois. I asked the builder about them, as well as other people from the area, and everyone told me not to worry, because there hadn't been a hurricane in this area of Florida since 1960. Well this was 2004, and this turned out to be a banner year for hurricanes in Florida. We were only in our home one week when Hurricane Charley decided to pay a visit. They do keep you informed as to where they think they are going to hit land, but Charley had a mind of his own. All during the previous day they said it was going north of us toward Tampa, but then it made a hard right turn toward us. The house came with hurricane shutters that were made out of galvanized steel panels, but they take some time to put up. Since we thought it wasn't going to come anywhere near us, like everyone else in our area we didn't put up the shutters right away. Now it was dark outside, and they expected Charley's arrival the next day. So, I was out there putting up hurricane shutters for the first time in the dark. Just as I finished putting them up, the wind started to kick up. We were as safe as we were going to be.

My brother that had lived in Charleston all those years, and had the experience of a few hurricanes behind him called me, and told me to fill my bath tub with water, because I may need it later. He also had some other advice, but at this point it was too late. Of course they recommend that you have a good supply of batteries, drinking water, canned goods, and so forth. Later I found out you should have a hurricane box to take with you if you have to evacuate. This would contain important papers, including insurance policies. You also need to have your cars filled up with gas, and you should have some cash on you. The reason for this is that if you lose power in your area gas pumps won't work, and ATMs need power to operate for cash, and credit cards won't be used either. I did learn one thing independently, and that is should have at least one corded phone because although we lost power we never lost our phone lines, and only a corded phone would work.

We were very fortunate, and didn't sustain any damage, other than having a palm tree pushed over by the wind. There had been four hurricanes pass through Florida that year, and many people are still trying to put their lives back together. All during the hurricane, while we were encapsulated inside our home, I had the feeling that I was back in a bunker again. I tried to find a place where I could look out, but it was dark, and with the wind howling outside there was a sense of familiarity. Maybe it was the stress of the situation, or the appearance of my surroundings, but I have found over the years that any stress at all, puts me back in Vietnam

Shortly after all the hurricanes left us, I received an e-mail out of the clear blue. It was from Fergie, a guy that had been with me in Vietnam. He saw my name on a military website where I had written something previously. He asked me if I was the same guy that had served with him in Vietnam. So, I replied to his e-mail, and told him that I was one and the same, and left him my phone number. He called, and we had a long and emotional conversation. The last time he saw me was when I was getting ready to be sent home from the hospital in Vietnam. Based upon what he recalled, he figured that I was dead. He and Fang had come to see me in the hospital, and was sure that if I didn't die then, that I would surely be dead by now anyway. We talked about a lot of things, and other people that were there with us in that conversation. He asked me if I remembered a guy named Chuck, and that the two of them came to Vietnam together, and were real close friends over there. Then he said how much he would like to see him again, and wondered how his life went. I told him that I had some good news for him, not only did I know where Chuck lived, but I have his phone number. I had seen Chuck at the first reunion that I attended. I think this put Fergie in a state of shock. Anyway, after our conversation ended he called Chuck. A short time later he and his wife were on a plane from Arizona to Florida. Chuck also lives in Florida, but he is about a four hour drive from me. They went to Chuck's house, and stayed for a few days, and during this time we made arrangements for them to meet me in a place that was half way between our houses near Tampa.

I think this mini-reunion was one of the highlights of my life. You cannot imagine the feeling there was in finding each other after all these years. We just found a restaurant that didn't mind us sitting there for hours. We told them about our little story, and they took real good care of us. In fact our waitress had a brother in the Marine Corps that was going to Iraq.

We still talk frequently, and are planning another trip to get together again. This time it will be in Arizona. There were so many years where I could have used this support, but none of knew where the other ones were, and after so many years had passed, you wondered if any of them would remember you in the first place. Apparently I wasn't the only one that felt this way.

There are a still a number of guys that I remember that I would like to see again, such as Patrick, Big Charles, Louie, Willy, and everybody else that I have mentioned in this book. I don't know if they would remember me or not, but I would sure like to have the chance. Memory is a strange thing, we can only store so much, and even if we were part of the same experience, our memories may only recall some of the mutual experience that we shared together in the same manner. At the reunion I had a few people tell me that they remembered me, but for the life of me, I couldn't remember them, and this may be the case for some of the guys that I remembered. No matter what, I would still like the opportunity.

I regret not having written down the names, and addresses of those I served with early on. To try to recall this information nearly four decades later has become almost impossible. I have been fortunate to have at least made contact with a few. The other regret I have, is not attempting to make contact with the families of those that were lost. To be honest, I was probably more afraid of my own feelings at the time. I just don't know how it would have been received a short time after it happened, and I don't know how you could possibly lessen the pain for them anyway. At this later date would they even want to talk about it anymore, and would it only serve to open more painful memories for them, I guess it depends on the family. With the families I have made contact with in the last few years, the experience has been one of the most gratifying occasions I had ever experienced in my entire life, but there are probably just as many families on both sides of this equation.

There was one thing that I failed to consider when I made the plans to move. This would require that I would have to start all over again at a new VA facility. This would mean new Doctors, as well as new groups to attend. I was just getting used to the ones back in Illinois, and had made some progress. Now I had to explain everything all over again to people I didn't know. In the small therapy groups there are many guys that have gotten to know each other over a period of years in some cases, and now I was going to be walking into a group as a new guy again. I don't know if I had the strength to relive the same explanations of my experiences all over again. It was a very painful process the first time around. I haven't done much talking so far, and maybe it's just me, but I still feel like an outsider. I do go there every week, but it takes me hours of preparation to get   relaxed enough to walk through the door. I still arrive early, and listen to music out in the parking lot for a few hours before I go in.

All in all my life hasn't changed that much since I moved, but at least I can walk on the beach, enjoy the sunshine, and maybe even take fishing up again. Hopefully once I conclude this little writing project of mine I will get back out on the water again. There is a little irony in all this, I spent my whole life running away from my past, yet unable, and unwilling to leave it alone, and what did I run to, but a hot humid climate, not unlike the one I left in Vietnam, and maybe that was the plan all along, but my immediate surroundings are much different now. I still listen to my old Motown music, and it still brings back the memories, but now when I'm listening I try to remember only the good ones.

Chapter 17

Final Thoughts

I guess we all wonder from time to time what our lives would have been like, if we only had made a few different decisions along the way. Since our life is not on tape we can't rewind it, or go back to change the outcome, instead we go forward through life making what we hope to be good decisions at the time, and then we have to live with the consequences of those decisions, both good, and bad. There are outside factors that alter how we live, but in most cases, it is our own decisions that will have the greatest effect in what direction our life will take.

As a society, we also make decisions that affect the outcome of people's lives both individually, and collectively. This is what defines us as a society. In making these choices we try to do what is best for the common good of everyone, but no matter how well intentioned we are, the results aren't always equally distributed, and some will always be left out.

During time of war, history shows us that in most cases we have stood together and performed whatever sacrifices were necessary as individuals and as a country to win the outcome. During the Vietnam War we were a divided nation, both philosophically, and politically. There are people that believe these differences are a good thing, and are just our form of government in action. For those fortunate enough to be able to sit on the sidelines, and analyze these circumstances as they unfolded, life just consisted of a lively debate. To the people that were sent to fight in this war, life was quite different. This country had been divided before, and the greatest example of this was the Civil War. Ironically even with all the debate, and protests that were held as a result of our involvement in Vietnam, it became the longest lasting War in our nation's history. The people that were not involved in the war itself, have gone on with their lives, and have pretty much forgotten about it, while those that participated are in many cases still fighting, and trying to find their portion of the American Dream.

To all the Politicians of this country present, and future, please learn from this War. We cannot, and should not get involved in a War where the country itself doesn't feel the commitment to the cause. In doing so, you will only squander the youth of this country. One day you may have the need to call upon them to defend the very existence of this country, and if this history continues to repeat itself, there may not be anyone willing to step forward. You also have an obligation to them, as well as the rest of the country, to have a plan in place to win, and be committed to carrying it out. Also you must consider as part of the cost of participating in a war, the care you will need to provide the returning Veterans afterward. Their War won't be over just because you say it is, and this needs to be done before you send in the first man.

To the people of this country, you are represented by the Politicians that you elect. It is pitiful that so many people don't even participate in the election of whom they want to represent them. This is a conscious decision that you make, to not participate in your own future, or that of your family. People tend to live in a bubble in this country, and despite all the information available, we usually are only concerned with how our own lives are going to be impacted, and are oblivious to those around us. The attitude evoked is basically, if nothing in my life is affected, then I don't care, and don't want to get involved, even if all it means is casting a vote every so often. We do however demand our right to our opinion, yet when it counts we choose not to make it known. It's no wonder how we are perceived by the rest of the world.

To the Veterans of this country, I salute you. There is no greater service to one's country than the willingness to defend it. As Veterans we fall into the categories of the wars that we participated in. Our older Veterans fought in World War II, and Korea. Those of my age fought in Vietnam, and later we had men in the Gulf War. Today we have people fighting in Iraq, and Afghanistan. I would like to suggest to the younger Veterans that they stay in touch with each other. This will become more important to you later. You may be looking for some support someday that you will be unable to find anywhere else. As Veterans, we have some things in common, but our individual experience is our own, and no other Veteran of any era should ever put them self in the position of judging any other Veteran's experience.

To the families that suffered the greatest loss, there are many of us out there that share in your grief. We as Veterans, were the ones that bore witness to the event that took your loved ones away from you, and we will carry that memory with us for the rest of our days, and until we join them. No one can tell you how you should feel, or how much time the grieving process will take. We are all made differently, but one thing is clear, it has never been easy to lose one that you've loved so much to war.

Pictures

Me 1967

Chuck

Doc Ski

Fang

1967

Doc Ben K.I.A 4/21/1968

Lt. John K.I.A 4/21/1968

Little John
K.I.A 1966

My Squad
1967

*Hospital
1967*

Getting my purple heart

Fergie, Art

*Leaving for
Second Tour*

Patty

Patty, Me

Bonnie, Art, Me, Barb
—Doc Ben's Family

Acknowledgements

My Wife Patty: Thank you for your love, and support for nearly four decades. Without you I would never have had a life, or at least not one worth living.

My Daughters Kelly and Kerry: I am more proud of you than you will ever know, and have enjoyed watching you grow into the women you are today.

My grandchildren: You are the absolute light of my life, and I hope and pray your lives will never be touched by war

My Parents: Thank you for giving me such a great start in life and for the example you set as parents. I still miss you both very much.

My Brother Jim: Everyone could use the support of a big brother like you.

Art, Bonnie, Barb, Paula, Jo, and Jean: I cannot express in words, what your acceptance, and love has meant to me. God has blessed me with you

Art: I want to thank you for what you have done for me, and every veteran you have helped through the system

Paul: You were a good friend then, and I'm grateful to have renewed that friendship again.

Fergie: It was a shock to you, and a welcome surprise to me to have reconnected after all these years. Thank you for remembering me Buddy.

Chuck: Thanks for showing me that writing a book wasn't just a possibility, but could become a reality.

Clyde: You have been an inspiration to me, as well as to everyone else that has been given the opportunity to know you as a friend.

Doc Ski: Thanks for taking care of me and the rest of my buddies on top of that hill, when there was no one else to turn to.

Louie, Willy, Big Charles, Patrick, and the rest of the guys that I served with, hopefully we will find each other again someday

Lt. John, Doc Ben, Little John, Bud, Gary, Loren, and the rest who now sleep, your young faces are still in my mind, and the minds of many others. God Grant You Peace

Dr. John: Thank you for helping me through a difficult time in my life, and for all the efforts you've done to improve the lives of Veterans today.

My Old Groups from the VA in Illinois: Thanks for listening, and I look forward to visiting from time to time. Semper Fi

Burt: you were an old friend of mine when I really needed one, and taught me a lot about life and people.

Pastor Bill: Thank you for welcoming me with open arms after drifting for many years. You helped me find a piece of me that was missing.

My Old Crew at work: Thanks for making a job that was at times intolerable, more tolerable. I wouldn't have made it without you guys.

Oprah: Thank you! Being at your show helped me find my voice, and this book is the result of that experience.

Also available from PublishAmerica

A DEER IN WINTER
by Michelle Ordynans

A Deer in Winter is an inspiring story of survival. It's the semi-autobiographical tale of a young woman's odyssey as she escapes from an abusive home, endures homelessness in the cold of a New York winter, and survives sexual attacks and harassment. In the meantime, she continues her last term of high school while secretly homeless, in constant fear of being discovered and returned to her abusive household. Through it all, she sets her sights on meeting her ultimate goal— graduating high school and attending college in the fall so that she can eventually rise above her troubled background and build a better life for herself. All the rituals of daily life must be negotiated: how and where she sleeps each night, in the rain and snow; how she gets food; how she cleans herself and her clothes;

Paperback, 206 pages
6" x 9"
ISBN 1-4241-6999-2

and how she spends her evenings. Along the way she works, makes friends and boyfriends, and explores the fascinating sites of New York City.

About the author:

Michelle Ordynans was born and has lived in New York most of her life, with her early childhood in Florida and a few years in Israel. She is married and has two grown children and several pets. She works with her husband and son as an insurance broker in New York City.

Available to all bookstores nationwide.
www.publishamerica.com

THE GAME OF LIFE

by David Shiben

Why are we here? What is the meaning of life? Why is life so difficult? Why is the world in chaos? Why does God allow such bad things to happen to his people? Why don't we stop global warming? Can we ever have peace on earth?

About the author:

David is just shy of the big 5-0. He was raised Lutheran/Presbyterian. Early in life he questioned mainstream religion, thinking many of the good churchgoing people were hypocritical, praying for one hour on Sundays and doing whatever the rest of the week. They did not walk the walk or talk the talk. He also found that the church could not answer many of the big questions about life. David became disenfranchised with the church and wallowed through a number of difficult years. In the mid 1990s, David began to search for answers and started reading many self-help and spiritual books. He started meditating and began his communion with the Supreme Being and now answers these questions, explains living your life without fear, and inspires provocative ideas and solutions to many of the world's greatest problems—global warming, child abuse, war, prejudice, government, the legal system, and the like.

Paperback, 244 pages
6" x 9"
ISBN 1-4241-9914-X

Available to all bookstores nationwide.
www.publishamerica.com

Also available from PublishAmerica

TUNNEL OF DARKNESS
by Rose Falcone De Angelo

Why are some people given the ability to see into the future or communicate with the dead? Is this a gift or a curse? The visions come uninvited and change an ordinary world into one of marvel, turmoil and sometimes fear. This is the story of Bernadette, whose psychic powers begin at the age of ten and carry her into the strangest places.

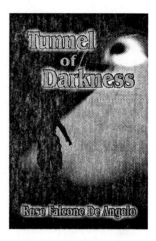

Paperback, 241 pages
6" x 9"
ISBN 1-60474-153-8

About the author:

Rose Falcone De Angelo was born in New York City's east side to Italian immigrant parents. Rose moved to Florida in 1986. She is the author of a book of poetry, *Reality and Imagination*. At ninety-one, she is the oldest published poet in the state of Florida and has intrigued all who have the privilege of knowing her. She is currently working on her memoirs.

Available to all bookstores nationwide.
www.publishamerica.com